Passive Income ... ~.......~ Your Life:

How to Work Less and Make More Money

By

Sam Kerns

Books by Sam Kerns

How to Work from Home and Make Money: 10 Proven Home-Based Businesses You can Start Today (Work from Home Series: Book 1)[1]

How to Build a Writing Empire in 30 Days or Less (Work from Home Series: Book 2)[2]

How to Start a Home-Based Food Business: Turn Your Foodie Dreams into Serious Income (Work from Home Series: Book 3)[3]

How to Brand Your Home-Based Business: Why Business Branding is Crucial for Even the Smallest Startups (Work from Home Series: Book 4)[4]

How to Publish a Book on Amazon: Real Advice from Someone Who's Doing it Well (Work from Home Series: Book 5)[5]

The Writer's Toolbox Boxed Set (Work from Home Series)[6]

The Weekend Writer: How to Write a Non-Fiction Book in 2 Months, Even if You Have a Full-Time Job (Work from Home: Book 6)[7]

---

1. https://goo.gl/ksYZY3

2. https://goo.gl/C5Eiq7

3. https://goo.gl/mE2nYT

4. https://goo.gl/6flLFo

5. https://goo.gl/jYSZlH

6. https://goo.gl/hKKhsG

7. https://goo.gl/FhHHOh

How to Relaunch Your Book: Use This Step-By-Step Proven Program to Bring Your Book Back to Life (Work from Home: Book 7)[8]

The 30-Day Work from Home Challenge: Do You Have What it Takes to Be Your Own Boss, Be Successful, and Make Money? (Work from Home: Book 8)[9]

Passive Income Will Change Your Life: How to Work Less and Make More Money (Work from Home: Book 9)[10]

Sign up at RainMakerPress.com[11] to receive advanced notice of new books in the series!

8. https://goo.gl/QvWWvr

9. https://goo.gl/oWPKD1

10. https://amzn.to/2rZPPQC

11. http://www.rainmakerpress.com/

What is Passive Income and How Will It Change Your Life?

Common wisdom says there are two paths people can take in their financial lives. First, you can work for someone else and help build their portfolio, savings account, and dreams by being a good and loyal employee. But studies have shown that it's almost impossible to build wealth while working for someone else.

Your other traditional choice is to start your own business. It's definitely better than working for someone else because owning your own business gives you more control over your life, and it's a great way to build wealth. But if you've read any of my books about starting a small business, you know that it's not an easy task. In fact, studies confirm that when you work for yourself, you will work more hours than if you held a 9 to 5. But financial rewards do await those who are persistent and smart.

But there is a third way to build wealth that isn't talked about as much: passive income. Unfortunately, there is a lot of bad information about the topic. For example, if you Google it, you'll find articles about earning passive income by using cash back credit cards, or signing up for programs that give small amounts of cash every time you shop using their app. And while those are perfectly legitimate ideas, they aren't exactly paths to financial wealth.

In this book, I'm NOT going to teach you how to earn enough passive income to buy a good meal every now and then. I'm going to teach you how to use passive income to gain financial freedom.

But that's not the only thing that I will address in this book.

When seeking information about passive income ideas, you will find a lot of bad information. For instance, some people say passive income requires zero effort on your part. But the reality is that there is no such thing as a purely passive income stream. Every single dollar you make from passive income requires *some* work, even if it's just five minutes to set it up. (More about this in a minute)

Why Did I Write this Book?

The books in my Work from Home series have so far focused on opening a small business. I've taught you how to know if you're ready to start a business, how to brand a small business, how to open a writing business, how to start publishing books, how to open a cottage food business, and how to write a book only on weekends, and how to relaunch a book that isn't selling. I've written so many books about entrepreneurship because it's my passion. I am a serial entrepreneur who firmly believes that running your own business is one of the only pathways to personal and financial freedom.

But what I've neglected to tell you in my other books is that I don't always trade my time for money. A lot — if not most — of my income is passive.

And so when my twenty-one-year-old son asked me to teach him about earning passive income, I had an epiphany. Why not use my knowledge and turn it into a book that teaches him everything I know? But after thinking about it, I came to the conclusion that everyone, not only my son, needs to understand what passive income is and how to use it to build a better life.

So while I wrote this book as a financial love letter to my son, you will also get the benefit of learning what you need to know to begin earning passive income so you can build a better life.

Forget everything you've heard so far about earning passive income. While most books on the topic only provide lists of passive income ideas, mine is different. Instead of offering you 100 ideas on the topic — with no information that allows you to pursue the ideas — I have written in-depth about 12 passive income ideas.

Why only 12?

Because all of the passive income ideas in this book are big. I don't play around with ideas that will only earn you a couple of bucks here and there. I want you (and my son) to use this knowledge to help move you from the 9 to 5 lifestyle to financial freedom. So if you're looking for passive streams of income that produce big results, you've found the right book.

For each idea, I'll give you an in-depth look at what it is, the income potential, and then offer a detailed outline showing you how to begin earning passive income from it. I'll give you all the information you need, including the necessary resources and a step-by-step program for each of the ideas to help jumpstart your path.

But here's the thing: not all passive income is easy. I know it sounds like it should be, but it's not — at least not at first. But after you've set up your streams of income, the rewards are rich, trust me. But to get there you will need to do a little work *in the beginning*. But don't worry because I'll show you exactly how to do that as we go along.

Are you ready? We have a lot to cover, which is why this book is longer than most of my others. But before we get into the 12 passive income streams, I'd like to start out by telling you why wealthy people refuse to trade their time for money and instead rely on passive income streams.

Chapter One: Why Wealthy People Don't Work for Their Money

Have you ever noticed that wealthy people seem to have a lot of time on their hands? They have time to go to their kid's games or plays, they can take a vacation any time they want, and if they want to pursue a hobby, they have the freedom to do so.

So, what' the difference between those people and most of the other people in the world? The wealthy refuse to trade their time for money.

Most people have a job, and that means they have to show up to work every day. In exchange for doing this, they get paid, either by the hour or with a monthly salary. And while many people consider this a necessary part of life, I'm here to tell you it's not.

Here's why.

When you trade your time for money, you limit the amount of money you can earn. And that's true no matter how much money you make.

The key to earning passive income is to trade *less* of your time for *more* money. Let me give you a brief example. (We'll talk more about this later in the book.)

If you make $50,000 a year working for someone else, your hourly rate is $25. (To figure your rate, divide your yearly income by two and then take away three zeros. 50,000 / 2 = 25,000 = $25 an hour)

That means if you worked a crazy 70 hours per week, the maximum amount of income you could earn is $7,000 a month or $84,000 a year. (Working 52 weeks a year)

But to earn that $84,000, you would have to work 3,640 hours a year. (People who work a 40-hour week "only" work 2,080 hours a year.)

And all those extra hours won't contribute to a happier life, either. Sure, you would be able to pay the bills easier and maybe send your family off on a nice vacation (You won't be able to go—remember you're tied to a desk 70 hours a week.)

But everyone has their limits, and that's where trading your time for money hits a brick wall. Let's say our imaginary person wanted to earn $10,000 a month to afford the lifestyle he and his family dreams of. To make it happen, he would have to work 100 hours a week.

Can you imagine? That barely leaves enough time for sleep, let along family, hobbies, or relaxation.

Crazy, huh?

Are you getting the picture? When you trade your time for money, you quickly become entangled in a trap. You have to put in the work to earn enough money, but then you don't have enough time to enjoy it. And if you need to earn even more money? You guessed it—you will have to work even more hours.

There is a Way Out of the Rat Race

Before you resign yourself to a life of all work and no fun, let me show you the other side of the equation. What if you had a passive income stream? It may look something like this:

Passive income stream: online course:

An initial 900 hour investment = $20,000 a month income, or $240,000 a year.

That's $120 an hour and you would work 2,460 fewer hours that year.

Notice that all of the work done on this income stream is front-loaded. You do the work up front, and then collect the rewards for as long as people continue to buy your course. Sure, you may need to update the course occasionally, but that shouldn't take more than a few hours.

Do you see how working less and earning more money can give you the freedom you want? It's the mindset of the rich — they can do what they want with their lives because they have passive streams of income flowing in. In other words, they don't work for their money: their money works for them.

Another problem with putting all of your eggs in the "job" basket is that sometimes the economy — or the company you work for — takes a hit and you could find yourself out of a job. Just ask all the people who lost their jobs in 2008 and had to give up their homes and cars. When you only rely on one stream of income and you lose it, it means disaster — unless you have more income streams to count on.

The 7 Streams of Income of Millionaires (Plus One)

So, what's the answer? Multiple streams of passive income. Research shows that wealthy people have on average seven streams of income. When you have a diversified stream of income, you have a lot more options, and bumps in the road such as a corporate layoff or sluggish economy won't affect you as much.

So, what are the seven streams of income that most millionaires have? They are all different of course, but here are the most common. (I've included an extra one because I believe it's a significant source of income for those who are willing to do it the right way.)

Earned Income

This is the income where you *do* trade your time for dollars. It is your job. For example, if you work for $25 an hour, that is your first stream of income. Obviously, this isn't passive income, and your goal will be to eventually replace this income with your passive income streams.

But not everyone wants to give up their earned income streams of revenue. For example, you may love your job and plan to work at it until you retire. But that doesn't mean you don't need alternative streams of income as a safety net. Just ask any millionaire who continues to work at their job. You can bet they have other streams of income to boost their net worth.

Profit Income

When you start a business, you will earn a profit on the goods you sell or the services you provide. For example, if you start an online store, the sales you make — less your expenses — are your profit income. And if you run a service business such as plumber business, the profits you earn from those calls — less your expenses, including what you pay the plumbers — are your profit.

We will talk about this is the chapter about starting business. And for those of you who are already calling me on the carpet for including information about starting a business in a book about passive income — hold on. I've got a new way of looking at it that will make you see things differently.

Interest Income

When you lend your money to someone else, the interest you charge them is considered interest income. I have a lot to say on this increasingly easy and profitable way of earning passive income later in the book. (And no, you don't need a lot of money to get started!)

Stocks and Dividend Income

Some stocks pay out dividends on a monthly or quarterly basis. Those dividends are a form of passive income. But even those stocks that don't pay out dividends are a great source of passive income because of the magic of compound interest. I'll explain how getting started with as little as $500 today can fund your retirement.

Rental Income

Don't even get me started. I will spend a lot of time on this subject because it has proven to be so profitable for me. Most people think about renting their house, and that is a fantastic way to make passive income, but there are so many more great options. Stay tuned...

Capital Gains

When you own stock in a company that is doing well, the value of your stocks increase. This increase is how many people earn passive income.

Royalty Income

This is another passive income stream that is near and dear to my heart. You can make a killing with royalty income. And here's the thing: once you create a product that people want (and keep it updated), you can earn royalties from it for years to come. That's true whether you create eBooks, e-learning courses, music, or art.

Affiliates and Paid Advertising

Affiliates get a bad rap because so many people get sucked into get-rich schemes associated with them. But affiliate passive income is real. The difference between people who earn real passive income from it and those who don't is the amount of time they put into it. By starting a blog and using paid advertising and affiliates, you can build a substantial passive income stream. More on how to do this later.

Each of these passive income streams can bring money into your household with little effort from you. Yes, you will have to do some work to set them up, but after that, it's like getting free money every month.

The great thing about all these streams of income is that you can do them part time, and most don't take a lot of money to get started. So, although you don't have to be a millionaire to cash in on these profitable streams of income, you can use the same methods and strategies that they do to build wealth. And who doesn't love that?

But before we delve into all the ways you can automate your income, let's tackle a few myths and misconceptions about passive income streams.

Chapter Two: The Myths and Misconceptions About Passive Income Streams

With something as promising as passive income streams, there are bound to be myths and misconceptions about the process. In fact, many of the false ideas about passive keep honest people from pursuing them.

I've outlined some of the more prevalent falsities about the method below. Once you have a good understanding of what passive income is *not*, you will be better able to take advantage of what it *is*.

Passive Income is 100 Percent Passive

That's an enticing thought, isn't it? The idea that you can start receiving an income stream without lifting a finger is what many people think of when they consider passive income. But that's just plain wrong.

Passive income always takes some work to set up. You may spend a few days researching stocks when planning to invest, or you may spend 900 hours to build an e-learning course like in the example above. While it's not passive when setting it up, *it becomes passive when you launch it.*

It's not realistic to believe that you don't have to do anything to begin earning a wealth-building stream of income.

I understand that this myth will burst a lot of people's bubbles. I've seen the negative comments left on blogs and YouTube videos for people who try to explain this fact, but I'm not writing this book to earn fans. I'm writing it to teach you (and my son) how to build your wealth with passive income. And I'm nothing if not honest.

But if you're still somehow stuck in the belief that you can earn a great income without lifting a finger, please read the next chapter about passive income scams before you invest all your hard-earned money in a system that won't work.

To drive home the point, here's the difference between passive income and earned income. With passive income, you do the work upfront and then sit back and collect the fruits of your labor. The money you earn from doing some upfront work could last a lifetime.

On the other hand, when you collect earned income, it's always in exchange for your ongoing time. You may go to work every day to earn a paycheck, or run a business. If you don't put in the time, you won't earn the money. And there is never a resting period where you only collect the money.

Passive income can be summed up like this: Do the work, then sit back and enjoy the fruits of your labor.

You Need a Lot of Money to Earn Passive Income

Again, this just isn't true. There are many paths to earning passive income, and they all take varying amounts of money. But here's the thing: you can start as small you want and scale up.

And there are some passive income ideas you can pursue without any money at all.

In later chapters, I will go into great detail about how much each of my passive income ideas take to get started, and how you can increase your investments in them as you go.

You Can Set up a Passive Income Stream Overnight

The too-good-to-be-true hucksters will tell you that you can set up a stream of passive income in a day and then only think about it when you get your monthly checks. Unfortunately, this myth also sets people up for failure and disappointment.

If you want to develop serious streams of passive income, you will need to research each stream, set it up properly, and maintain it. Anything other than that is just a pipe dream.

For example, blogs are a great form of passive income because you earn affiliate income, advertising income, revenue from books, products, or online courses. But a blog has to be set up properly and maintained. You will need to research and set up the affiliates and advertisers, write the books, develop or find the products you offer, create the online courses, add new content to your blog, occasionally update your offerings, and reach out to your mailing list every now and then. Is the income mostly passive? Yes, because you aren't trading your time for money, but are reaping the profits from a business set up and run properly. But you can't set up a successful blog overnight.

You Only Need One Stream of Passive Income

It might be tempting to only develop one stream of passive income but that can get you in trouble. For example, think about the people who invested in the stock market as their only passive income stream in 2008. Much of their wealth and dividends were wiped out in an instant. That's why millionaires have seven streams of passive income. If one fails, you will continue to collect from the others.

But you need to be smart in how you approach this. I recommend starting with one stream of income, and once it is up and running correctly, start on your second one. Remember, to truly earn good revenue streams, you will need to carefully construct them. And building them one by one will ensure that you put in the time necessary to develop them correctly. That's how you will earn the most amount of money from each income stream.

Passive Income Streams are Permanent

Another common myth that can get you into serious trouble is that once you set up your passive income streams, you'll continue collecting the checks forever. But that's not how it always works out.

Things change, and just because you're making a substantial monthly income from a passive income stream, that doesn't mean it will last. For example, I have a good friend who developed an extensive website. He sold SEO content and created a labyrinth of articles that Google indexed well. He made a LOT of money from affiliates, advertising, and the money people paid him to produce the content. (He outsourced everything).

Then one day, Google changed its algorithms and he lost it all. He went from a hugely successful business to almost no income at all.

Do you see why it's so important to develop more than one stream of passive income? And even if yours is generating a lot of income, don't sit back and count on it to stay that way forever. You need to be on top of your game and constantly look for new passive streams of income to add to your portfolio. I can assure you that my friend wishes he had taken this advice.

Any Passive Income Idea Will Work

Finally, too many people believe they can latch on to just any passive income idea and it will work for them. But there is a flaw in this thinking.

Any passive income idea will work — for the right person. It's important that you honestly evaluate your skill set before embarking on a passive income idea. For instance, if you love the idea of generating royalties from book sales, it's important that you carefully assess your ability to write a book. Just because you publish a book, that doesn't mean you will generate revenue from it. It must be well-researched and written for readers to buy it.

The same is true for any passive income stream you pursue. Passive income ideas all work — but not for everyone. Just be honest when examining each idea to determine if you're ready to pursue that idea or if you need to learn some new skills or get some experience first.

Are you still with me? I realize that these myths and misconceptions may be the complete opposite of what you've heard before, but they're true. The scammers and hucksters have completely twisted the idea of passive income that a great majority of people now believe it's possible to get rich without lifting a finger.

But that's not how it works.

Does that make earning passive income any less desirable? Not at all. I love getting my passive income every month and will continue to build my streams. But I understand that for each passive income stream I build, I will have to put in some upfront work and then maintain it.

That beats schlepping to the office every day to trade my time for money.

If you want to build serious wealth with passive income streams, you have to approach it seriously. Leave the get rich overnight schemes to those who want something for nothing and don't understand what it takes to build true financial wealth.

In fact, it would be enlightening to those dreamers in a couple of years. You can compare your success after building passive income streams the right way to their pie-in-sky dreams. Chances are, they will be right where they started — reading the latest get rich quick scheme and talking about how it's going to change their life. You, on the other hand, will be quietly collecting income checks from the passive income streams that you set up the right way.

Now that you understand how passive income really works, I'd like to teach you about some passive income scams that you should avoid.

Chapter Three: Passive Income Scams and How to Avoid Them

I believe in the merits of passive income. It has made my life a lot easier because I'm able to earn monthly income without spending a lot of time on it. (But remember, I *did* spend time on my streams of income initially!)

But what I don't believe in is how scammers are exploiting innocent people into believing that passive income is something that it's not. Every day, someone becomes a victim to a scammer who promises them they can earn a lot of money for doing nothing.

That's why I want to talk to you about passive income and scams. I want you to be able to quickly identify passive income scams and heresy so you will never get sucked into a scammer's web of lies.

Pyramid Schemes

Have you seen the ads for companies saying that you too can drive a brand new car, live on a yacht, or own an expensive vacation home by signing up for their program? They are a dime a dozen, and most of them are pyramid schemes. But they're often passed off as passive income opportunities.

Pyramid schemes have been around forever, but lately they've taken a new twist. The people who are running them are trying to cash in on the passive income trend, and are trying to convince people that they can earn a huge income by simply signing people up to their program.

But think of the structure of a pyramid: it's narrow on the top and very wide on top. And it's the perfect symbol of how these organizations operate. Those people at the top — the founders of the pyramid scheme and those who entered the program in the early days — earn money for everyone else who later signs up to the program because they get a portion of the signup fee. They are indeed making a lot of money — off of other people's backs.

Each person that signs up to a pyramid scheme enters at a lower level and will earn less money than those who signed up before them. And eventually the money runs out because people figure out that it's a scam.

How does this relate to passive in income? Because of the way it's sold.

Here's a breakdown of how pyramid schemes work and the way they get people to part with their hard-earned money.

They approach people and tell them that they have a new money-making system that will allow them to earn money without putting in a lot of time or work. All you have to do is tell other people about this "exiting opportunity" and get them to join up. When they do, you will earn a portion of their signup fee. Oh yeah, did I forget to mention that? You need to pay hundreds of dollars to join this amazing organization.

So you pay your join up fee, and a portion of it goes to the person who recruited you. The person who recruited them gets a cut as does the person who recruited them. You don't get anything for your money because pyramid schemes don't sell products — they only sell memberships.

Now it's your turn to start recruiting. You sign up your friends and family and anyone else who will listen and you get a cut of their sign up fees. And on and on it goes. The thing is, the scheme isn't based on a product or service, so it eventually fails. And those who come in at the end don't get anything in return for their signup fees.

Did I mention that pyramid schemes are illegal?

Pyramid schemes are not legitimate forms of passive income and you should avoid them like the plague. If you do make money on them, you're doing so at the expense of another vulnerable person.

Here's how to you tell if your "passive income" opportunity is a pyramid scheme.

- You are invited to join a great new company where you will earn a lot of money without having to work much.
- The company doesn't actually sell any products or services. If they do offer products (this is rare, but it happens), you will be told that while you can earn money selling products, the real income comes from signing up other people to sell.
- If the company sells products, they are unrealistically

priced.

- You will hear a lot of vague promises about the potential money you can make but no hard facts to back it up
- You are asked to pay a monthly fee for belonging to the program

In short, if the "opportunity" mostly involved getting other people to sign up for it, it's probably a pyramid scheme and you should run the other way.

Auto-Pilot Funnel Scams

Affiliate income is real, and I'm going to show you how to set up legitimate affiliate networks later that can earn you real cash. But some unscrupulous scammers have invented ways to lure in unsuspecting people into spending hundreds of dollars on "affiliate" programs.

Let me give you an example of how they work. You find a website that claims it can teach you how to make $500 a day with its exclusive program. All you have to do is pay a small fee (usually under $50) and you'll learn how to begin earning that kind of money. And the best part? The income is passive. In other words, you won't have to do anything to rake in that $500 a day.

As soon as you input your credit card number and sign up, you'll be presented with an upsell offer. You can now choose between spending a couple hundred dollars to a thousand to get the "exclusive" information that only the select have access to. If you agree, you are now on the hook for a lot of money.

Once you've forked over your money, you are given a few PDF files that teach you how to set up a squeeze page, which is nothing more than a WordPress site that allows people to buy stuff from you. You may even receive a plugin for your new site to make collecting money from other people even easier.

You will be given instructions about how to use SEO and other internet marketing techniques to drive people to your new site.

In other words, you will set up a site just like the one you've just bought from. Congratulations, you've just paid someone almost a thousand dollars to learn how to scam others.

If this passive income scam seems reminiscent of the envelope stuffing scams of yesteryear, you're right. It's the same scam, but it uses modern technology and passes itself off as a passive income opportunity.

Marketing and Affiliate Funnels

The last passive income scam I want to tell you about involves affiliate links and marketing funnels. Here's how it works. A website claims that if you follow its affiliate marketing plan, you can make hundreds of dollars a day. All you have to do is become a part of the marketing funnel and then you will earn money on the affiliate links that are a part of it. And it's free — what do you have to lose?

So, you decide you want to get involved in this great opportunity and click on the Get Started button. You find out that you need to sign up for all of the affiliate links that you will be earning commissions on, but here's the thing: you have to buy the products to sign up to become an affiliate. Some of the prices aren't so bad. You will pay under $50 for some of them, a monthly fee for others, but some cost in the hundreds of dollars. But, you keep reading how much passive income you will earn from the program so you pay the fees.

You are now an official member of all the affiliate programs. And the person who runs the site just earned affiliate commissions for everything you paid for. And here's the thing: you don't need to purchase a product to become an affiliate for it. But the person who runs the site needed to make money off of you and that's how they tricked you into it.

Now you are given the opportunity to set up your own website page, which is a part of the one you were just scammed on. Your job as the owner of this new page is to send people to your website page and give them the same promises. And every time someone signs up, you will get a portion of the affiliate fee, but the person who owns the original website will also take a cut. After all, your website page is attached to theirs.

Here's the Good News: You Can Earn Legitimate Passive Income

I realize that the picture I just painted for you is distressing. After all, if you only knew about these types of passive income "opportunities," you may be tempted to believe that you have to scam other people to make passive income.

Fortunately, that's only the dark side of the process. Just as in any area, scammers are taking advantage of people who don't understand what passive income really is. They go after those who want to make a lot of money without any real effort and they bilk them out of hundreds — or even thousands — of dollars.

But you won't fall into that trap now that you understand how they do it.

Next, I would like to talk to you about how to get the passive income mindset. As you learned in this chapter, the desire for passive income has to go beyond wanting to make money for doing nothing. You have to understand what it is, how it can change your life, and then decide what you are willing to invest in the process to reach financial freedom.

I'm going to get real in the next chapter and talk about why your mindset is important, and if you don't have the right one, how to get it.

Chapter Four: How to Build a Wealth-Building Mindset

Do you want to know the difference between someone who enjoys a life of financial freedom and someone who is always chasing the dollar? It's the ability to not only earn a lot of money, but also to *keep* it. Almost anyone can earn money, but those who understand how to keep it will enjoy the lifestyle we're talking about in this book.

Just ask all those lottery winners or famous people who had millions of dollars and are now flat broke.

And when you're talking about earning passive income streams, your mindset is more important than ever. That's why I want to talk to you about creating the right mindset when thinking about pursuing passive income ideas. Because if you don't, all your hard work in setting up the streams could turn out to be for nothing.

You see, some people sabotage their financial lives and aren't even aware of it. And until you recognize the behavior and change it, it won't do you any good to build passive income streams.

Please don't be tempted to skip this chapter. Even if you believe you would never sabotage yourself financially, read through this chapter and make sure you don't have any hidden traits you need to address.

Here are six ways we sabotage our financial lives — and how to overcome them and build a passive income mindset.

I Don't Deserve to Have Money

One of the biggest reasons people don't achieve financial freedom is because they don't believe they deserve to have success. This can come from how you were raised or beliefs that you developed along the way. Here are some underlying beliefs that contribute to this type of financial self-sabotage.

- If you don't work hard for your money you don't deserve it
- You need to punish yourself for something you've done in the past
- You can't justify having financial freedom when other people have to work so hard

I'm going to illustrate this with a personal story.

I have a brother who is not at all responsible with his money. He spends like he is the richest man in the world, but in reality, doesn't have much to his name. When our father passed away, he left us all an inheritance.

While my other siblings made investments and put the money to good use, my brother went through his in a year — and basically spent it on nothing. We kept trying to persuade him to invest in real estate or some other vehicle that would earn him a return on his investment, but he refused. When his money was gone, he said he felt relieved. He just didn't feel comfortable having all that money.

I'm not making this up.

If you're reading this book and you have these types of feelings, I want you ask yourself a question. You obviously believe that passive income and wealth are good for some people, so why are you different?

The key to overcoming the feeling of unworthiness is to identify the origin of the problem. Were you told as a child that you were no good? Did your spouse leave you for someone else, or are you married to someone who belittles you so often that you've started to believe it?

Whatever the reason, if you want to stop self-sabotaging yourself financially and finally break free so you can feel good about growing your wealth, you will need to face those beliefs head on. I recommend talking to a counselor or reading some books on the subject, but the bottom line is this: if you sabotage your finances, it doesn't matter how many passive income streams you build, they won't work. Because you will unconsciously ensure that they don't.

It's Too Much Work

A recent report shows that 74 percent of Americans have not saved enough money for retirement. And another report shows that even people who have a company-matched 401K plan only contribute a little more than 6 percent to that plan.

Yet, social security only pays out an average of $1,300 a month. Can you live on that?

What's the different between people who have accumulated millions in their retirement portfolios and those who haven't saved anything? Is it a difference in salaries? Available money to save?

No, it's effort. Because here's the truth: if you begin putting away as little as $20 a month into a 401K when you're young, you will have hundreds of thousands of dollars by the time you retire. But many people don't want to do the work to research the right 401K fund or take the time to transfer the money every month.

And that's a shame.

The same mindset gets people into trouble when it comes to developing passive income streams. I've already talked to you about the fact that passive income streams do take work. You have to put in the upfront hours and then maintain the stream. Unfortunately, many people are simply unwilling to put in the time or work.

And those people will never — and I mean never — build wealth.

If you still feel that you can get rich with little to no effort, I highly recommend putting down this book because you're not going to like my advice. There's a reason most wealthy and successful people laugh at get rich schemes: they don't work.

You want to Look and Feel Rich

There is a prevailing belief out there that rich people look rich. They only wear designer clothes and drive the most expensive cars. But as William Danko pointed out in The Millionaire Next Door[1], the rich aren't doing the things we think they are. He interviewed the everyday millionaires and found that most of them live beneath their means and optimize wealth-building strategies to grow their net worth. What they *don't* do is invest in expensive cars and designer clothing. It turns out that's only a subset of the wealthy — the ones who flaunt their wealth on television and social media.

If you want to earn passive income streams to impress your friends and family by buying expensive toys, you need to re-think your mindset.

Most people with money understand that the value of the money is worth far more than what it can buy. They ask themselves questions during the course of their lives like this one:

I could buy that $100,000 car, or I could use the money to invest and create a stream of passive income. Which one would enable me to continue living my lifestyle? Which one would allow me to leave a financial legacy to my children? Which one will earn me money instead of causing my bank balance to depreciate?

As you can see, buying a $100,000 car won't get you much in the way of long-term goals.

---

1. https://www.amazon.com/gp/product/B00CLT31D6/
   ref=as_li_tl?ie=UTF8&tag=aprigere-20&camp=1789&cre-
   ative=9325&linkCode=as2&cre-
   ativeASIN=B00CLT31D6&linkId=6003637168de4a5eef23d92561666b3d

When thinking about creating passive income streams, think about your reasons for wanting to do it. Will you use the income to live life and invest in the future, or will you blow it all on things that don't hold value? Try asking yourself the same types of questions every time you think about spending money on things you don't really need.

We've talked about the three main ways people sabotage their financial lives, but there's more. I also want to share with you some of the ways you can build a mindset that allows you to create wealth.

The Millionaire Mindset

If you want financial freedom, you have to change the way you think. That's because the mindsets that keep the poor and middle class in a perpetual cycle of struggle are often so established they don't even recognize them or how they limit their choices.

If you to build wealth using passive income streams (or any way, really), you need to develop the mindset of the rich. Here's how they think:

Look Through a Long-Term Lens

People who don't have money tend to look at things from the short view, but people who build wealth look at things from a long-term perspective. For example, a short-term view makes people ask how they are going to pay their bills this month. But a long-term view asks how they can increase their income to double it by the next year.

And here's the deal: when starting out, you can use both short-term and long-term views to get you over the hump. For instance, you may *have* to think about how you're going to pay your bills this month, but don't stop there. Once you figure out this month, begin to think about how you can avoid getting into the same situation next month by thinking about long term goals: how you can increase your income.

In order to think long term, you will have to set goals — and stick with them. For example, if your goal is to double your income by this time next year, you may decide to pursue two high-return passive income streams. Next, you will have to create a step-by-step plan to initiate the streams, and then you will need to follow through. If all goes according to plan, by this time next year you won't have to worry about how to pay your bills — but how to invest all the money you made from your new income streams.

Embrace Delayed Gratification

Another big difference between the poor, the middle class, and the wealthy is an ability to delay instant gratification. It's the desire to have things right now that cause people to whip out their credit cards for that deal they can't pass up, or to buy a house or car that they can't really afford. The result of that is payments that take away their ability to invest in passive income streams.

On the other hand, the rich understand that they may have to delay gratification to achieve a long-term goal. They don't buy the expensive car because they're concentrating on using that money to build their investment portfolio. They won't get to drive the expensive car now, but will be able to retire comfortably and without financial worries.

They wait for the things that would give them comfort in the present time because they know doing so will eventually give them financial freedom.

And isn't that everyone's goal?

You Don't Have to Do Everything Yourself

If you're one of the few people in the world who hasn't yet read The Four-Hour WorkWeek[2] by Tim Ferriss, you're missing out. The premise behind the book is that when you try to do everything yourself, you limit your earning potential. After all, there are only so many hours in a day, right?

The rich agree with this sentiment. They understand that if you try to do everything yourself, you will spend a lot of time doing stuff that other people could do, and that will make you miss out on a lot of other opportunities. Plus, when you hire out portions of your workload, it allows you to scale.

I not only have personal experience with this philosophy, but I wrote a book about the process to teach others how to do it in the writing industry. But boy, some of the reviewers are apparently stuck in this mindset because they obviously could not

---

2. https://www.amazon.com/gp/product/0307465357/

ref=as_li_tl?ie=UTF8&tag=aprigere-20&camp=1789&cre-

ative=9325&linkCode=as2&cre-

ativeASIN=0307465357&linkId=d2f6c6a6f55810b94c5f493d66d572d4

understand the premise of the book. They read about scaling up a writing business and accused me of taking advantage of other people. By giving them full-time jobs.

Yep, I'm serious. (You can read the reviews here.)[3]

So, I know that this mindset is common and the people who have it don't realize how it's holding them back from financial gain.

When people get stuck in this mindset, they aren't likely to build multiple streams of passive income. That's because when it comes time to assign portions of their business to others to manage (the entire point of passive income), they're too afraid to do it. They either believe that no one can do it as well as they can, or (like the reviewers of my book), they believe that's it's somehow evil to scale up a business and hire people to do most of the work for you.

It's basic economics, people. The people of the world who build wealth don't do it themselves. Instead, they create jobs and allow those people to help them scale their business to build wealth.

And the same is true for most passive income streams.

Create Your Own Opportunities

Another misconception is that you have to wait until everything is perfect and an opportunity comes your way. But if you have that attitude, you may wait a very long time.

---

3. https://goo.gl/C5Eiq7

Wealthy people don't wait for opportunities to come to them; they create them. Sure, sometimes wealthy people have a great connections who bring them deals, but that's not how most of the wealth is generated.

It's created by people taking chances. By someone finally deciding that they are tired of living paycheck to paycheck and want more for themselves and their families.

It's about getting smart and looking for opportunities instead of passively sitting back and waiting for them to arrive on your doorstep.

That's what we'll talk about in this book. I'm going to present you with solid passive income opportunities that have worked well for others. And they can work for you too — if you're ready to break out of the rat race and start living live on your terms.

Chapter Five: What Will it Take to Get the Lifestyle of Your Dreams?

You're dreaming, right? You're imagining the day when you can wake up when your body does, and not because of the screeching alarm coming from your phone.

You think about being able to be there for your kids — and not only when your boss tells you it's okay.

You want to spend more time on your hobbies, but can't seem to find the time. You dream of the day when you can prioritize the activities that matter the most to you.

You're tired of striving every month just to pay the bills. You want your financial life to be easier and not have to spend so much time worrying about a lack of funds.

Guess what? You *can* live the life you want. In fact, if you take the steps to build several streams of passive income, your life *will* change.

But you have to go about it the right way.

Framing Your Ideal Life

> When building your passive income streams, you are in control of your destiny.

Before you begin building your passive income streams, let's figure out your goals.

You can determine how much you will increase your earnings every month because the more effort you initially put into each stream, the higher your monthly earnings will be.

For example, if you decide to build an online course and only put a few hours into it, your passive income from isn't going to be very significant. On the other hand, if you put the required 800 to 900 hours into it and give consumers a solid course, you'll do much better.

The same is true for every passive income stream you build. *Which is why you should only build one at a time*. Focus on the first one, get it right, and then go to the second one, and so on.

Anything less will just be a waste of time.

Okay, let's start this section by naming your number — what do you want to earn? Notice that I didn't ask you what you need to earn. You can earn what you need by taking a second job or starting a side-hustle.

But we're not talking about just getting by, are we?

I'm asking you what you want.

Let's go about it like this:

Start by adding up all of your monthly expenses. Include things like this:

- Mortgage or rent
- Homeowner's insurance
- Property taxes

- Car payment(s)
- Car insurance
- Total debt payments (credit cards, loans, etc.)
- Groceries
- Phone bill
- Internet bill
- Monthly gas
- Monthly utilities
- Clothing expense
- Childcare
- Eating out
- Entertainment
- Child support
- Charitable giving
- Lessons
- Anything else you pay monthly

That total is what you need to make in order to live. Chances are, you make at least that much at your 9 to 5, but if you're like most people, you still struggle. That's because your car breaks down, the refrigerator goes out, or your kid needs some money to go on a school trip.

Whatever the reason, you're struggling.

So, how much would it take to stop the struggle?

How much would it take for you to begin living *the life you really want*?

You have your baseline, so where do you go from there? Double it? Triple it? Quadruple it?

There is no right and wrong answer. Your number is your number. I encourage you to dream big, because remember your monthly earnings will depend on what type of and how many passive income streams you successfully set up.

Millionaires have seven.

How many do you want?

The Lifestyle Changes You'll Have to Make

Now that you have your number, let's talk about how the changes you are going to have to make to set up some profitable income streams. Because you can't continue as you've been living and expect to turn everything around.

You have to begin sacrificing a little now so you can live like you want to in a couple of years.

Here are the major things you will need to begin right now. (In addition to the mindset changes we talked about in the last chapter.)

Get Used to Saving

If you're going to build passive income wealth, the habit of reckless spending should be in the rearview mirror. While it's true that you don't need a lot of money to set up some of the passive income streams I talk about in this book, it's also true that some of them do.

And the more money you can save, the better financial position you will be in.

There are five stages of wealth, and before you begin on your passive income plan, you need to determine where you are. That's because your stage will determine how you need to approach building your passive income stream.

Stage One

If you're in this stage, you're barely scrapping by. You live paycheck to paycheck and can't imagine ever having extra money to invest in a passive income stream. Before you started reading this book, you thought maybe there was some magic formula that would pull you out of your position, but now you realize there isn't.

Don't worry. I will show you how you can pull yourself up out of the mire and get started building your wealth—despite your current lack of funds.

Stage Two

People in this stage have just begun to take their financial lives seriously. They have begun to pay off their debt and have started saving some money. They aren't there yet, but have woken up from a slumber and realized that it's up to them to plan for the future.

Stage Three

If you're in this stage, you've gotten very serious about socking away some money. While people in stage two may save ten percent of their income, you're saving upwards of 25 percent—maybe even more. You have a nice bank balance and don't blow your money on things you don't need.

You understand that a healthy bank balance will get you where you want to go—even if you don't have it quite yet.

Stage Four

The people who have reached stage four have made a significant discovery: compound interest. And one they understood its power to propel their lives into the next stratosphere, they never looked back.

If you haven't yet reached this stage, here's a brief primer on how compound interest works.

The Magic of Compound Interest

Compound interest plays an important role in building wealth. And we'll take advantage of its magical properties in some of our passive income strategies.

When you invest money, you earn interest on it. For example, if you invest $1,000 and get a 10 percent interest rate, you will have $1,100 after one year.

But if you leave the money in the account, you will earn interest on the initial balance and the interest the second year. And the year after that.

If you leave your money intake, compound interest can multiple your initial investment many times over. And it gets better every year because you have earned more interest.

This is one of the greatest tools you have in creating wealth.

You can't start earning passive income until you invest some upfront money. And typically (but not always), the more you initially invest, the higher stream of income you will earn.

So if you're not in the habit of saving your money, you need to start doing so now.

To start with, everyone should have 3 to 6 months of living expenses in savings. If you don't, make a plan to do that now.

You May Have to Get a Side Gig

If you're maxed out every month and don't have a dollar to spare, you may have to get a side gig to make your dream of earning passive income come true.

Here's the deal: you can invest a tiny bit of money in a passive income stream, but doing so may mean that it will take years before it begins producing. Or if you don't have any cash, you may have to skip some of the passive income ideas I talk about because they do take some money.

Please put aside the lie right now that you can start earning income with no work — and no money. It takes money to make money — that's true. Not a lot maybe, but some.

So, what do you do if you don't have any money saved up? Start a side gig and work until you do.

Remember, this isn't a book that sells you a big lie about how you can make a million dollars without lifting a finger. Instead, it's about how to change your life for the better by creating passive income streams.

But you have to work for it. That's just the way it is.

If you are maxed out every month and don't think you can come up with any money, think about starting one of these side gigs as a way to create quick cash flow and fund your dream of passive income:

- Become an Uber[1] or Lyft[2] driver
- Work with Amazon Mechanical Turk[3]
- Rent your car on Turo[4]
- Work as a part-time virtual assistant
- Work from home a search engine evaluator[5]
- Start a fiverr[6] gig

And when your passive income streams start producing a monthly profit, you should either save the money that you don't need to live on, invest it back into the stream, or start a new income stream.

How does this look in real life?

Let's say you need $3,000 a month to live and you presently earn $3,000 a month at your 9 to 5. Your first income stream

---

1. https://www.uber.com/

2. https://www.lyft.com/

3. https://www.mturk.com/

4. https://turo.com/

5. https://connect.appen.com/qrp/public/jobs

6. https://www.fiverr.com/

begins to pay out $500 a month. You can choose to put all $500 into a CD and earn interest on it (a form of risk-free passive income), or reinvest it into the same stream. For example, if this stream is dividends from stocks, you can reinvest the dividends back into the stocks, which would ultimately result in a higher payout every month. Or you can start a completely new passive income stream with the $500.

Or let's say that you only make $2,800 at your 9 to 5, but need $3,000 to live. In that case, you should use $200 from the $500 to live, and use the remaining $300 for one of the same options listed above.

Notice that one of your choices was not to buy a new car or take a vacation.

Your goal is to build wealth, not buy fancy things, remember?

Once you set up a home for your savings, such as a CD, the stock market, or an REIT, don't touch it. One of the biggest mistakes I see people make is using their long-term savings for something today.

That's why you should have 3 to 6 months of living expenses in your account — you won't ever have to touch your wealth building account.

Hone in on Your Skills

Next, you need to take a hard look at what you're good at. While every passive income stream I talk about in this book is capable of earning a great stream of income, you should design your plan around the things you're good at.

After all, you will likely succeed at those things you enjoy and are good at. Here are some of the traits you can use to build profitable streams on income.

- Creativity such as writing books, making music, or creating art
- Management skills
- Developing ideas and concepts
- Investing
- Vision
- Building social media accounts and followers
- Blogging
- Tech

If you're proficient at any of the above, you can use those skills to help you build passive income.

Here's an example: I have creative skills, management skills, blogging skills, and I'm pretty good at conceptualizing and developing ideas and concepts. I have used those skills to develop passive income streams like this:

- Creative skills: to write this series of books (royalties as passive income)
- Management skills: to manage rental houses and run my mostly passive content business (rents and business profits as passive income)
- Blogging skills: to run my blog (affiliate income, advertising, and sales as passive income)
- Conceptualization skills: developing online courses (I'm in the process of doing this now and will collect

passive income from them soon.)
- Investing skills: Okay I really don't have these, but with today's online robo advisors, you don't need them. (passive income from 401K funds)

Even if you have skills that I haven't mentioned above, you can use them to create passive income. For example, if you are an expert at hunting game with a bow and arrow, or at creating unique cross stitching patterns, you can create an online course about the topic. And if you don't have tech skills? Hire someone to do it for you!

What about you? How can you use your strengths to create streams of income that will help you achieve the lifestyle you want?

Do the Research

Too many people invest in something before researching it or even understanding what it is. That's a great way to lose money.

When you're building income streams, you will need to understand each stream perfectly before investing a penny of your money in it. In other words, to make the most of your income streams, you have to understand how they work and how to best make use of them.

In this book, I'm going to break down 12 of them. I will provide you with all of the current research on each of them, the resources and information you need to get started on them, and even some general outcomes that other people have enjoyed from them.

But...ultimately, your success is up to you. Research my research. Challenge my assumptions. Make it your goal to prove me wrong and discover things I don't know.

You are the king of your passive income empire — take your rightful place and become the master of your universe. In other words, use the information I've provided, and take it even further.

I don't know about you, but I am ready to delve deep into the passive income streams I want to talk about. Remember, these aren't silly little schemes designed to provide you with a few extra bucks every month. Done right and these streams can seriously impact your monthly income.

Chapter Six: My Favorite Way to Earn Passive Income

I'm going to start our discussion about passive income with real estate because, in my opinion, it's the fastest way to build real wealth. And while it makes it easier if you have some money to get started, I will show you how to get it if you don't already have it.

First, let me tell you how I started earning passive income with real estate. We bought a house in a sleepy little beach town before the housing market began skyrocketing. It's largely a tourist destination, although a few thousand people live here. Our new home had an apartment on the bottom floor, and we decided to rent it out to cover our new mortgage.

That was the beginning of my real estate passive income journey. Since then, I've added another apartment to the house, making it a triplex, and collect $2,100 a month in passive income from 2 tenants. In the near future, I plan to rent out the top floor (where we now live) for another $2,500 a month, which will earn us a total of $4,600 in gross passive income from this one house.

And the passive income that these rentals create isn't the only way the house builds our wealth. We get free equity because the renters are paying off our mortgage. For example, we've had ten years of $2,100 a month in rentals on the beach house. That means our renters have paid $21,000 down on our mortgage, giving us that much more to add to the asset column of our balance sheet.

We plan to move a few hours north and buy a duplex or other type of house that has an on-property rental. This rental will also cover the mortgage and give us free equity on our new house.

Part of my success with this house was buying at the right time and taking advantage of the market. But deals like this exist all over the nation — you just have to find them. We'll talk about how later in this chapter.

Let me sum this up. In the almost ten years that we've owned the beach house, we've never paid the mortgage, utilities, property tax, or homeowners insurance. Our tenants have done that for us, plus some. And our new home will be set up the exact same way.

Can you see how real estate is a great tool for building passive income and wealth?

But there is so much to learn about this passive income stream. I'm going to focus on rentals because that's the only way real estate investing provides a monthly passive income stream. (Other than REITs, which we will talk about in another chapter.)

But before we dive into real estate as passive income, let me warn you about something to watch for in the real estate industry.

Real Estate Scams to Watch for

You've likely heard the commercials: "Come to our free real estate investing workshop and learn how you too can become an overnight millionaire!" One word of warning: don't go. Or if you do, at least have the right expectations.

The promotors of these seminars don't put them on to teach you the basics of real estate investing; they do it to make money. Here's the typical flow of how things go: you go to a free 2-hour seminar. They tell you about all of the passive income you could earn if you began a career in real estate investing. They show you the numbers, they introduce you to people who have done it, and those people tell you about the great lifestyle they're living because of their real estate investments.

They promise that you don't need any money to invest, and that you can purchase your first property within a week by following their program.

And then the seminar ends, and you're left hanging.

Wait, you say. I need that information in order to start investing in real estate and build this great new life! How could they end the program like this?

Not to worry, because for a few hundred dollars, you can continue learning all weekend. It's an upsell, and because they only gave you enough information to peak your interest during the free seminar, most people sign up.

So you spend the weekend learning some more about real estate investing. You learn that if you want to buy a house with no money, all you have to do is whip out your credit card and get a cash advance to use as a down payment. Or, how you can find a seller who is desperate enough that they will allow you take over their payments without giving them any upfront money.

Then, just as you think you're getting the hang of real estate investing, the weekend is over. You don't feel too bad — you did get some pretty good information for the money you spent. But you still don't feel prepared to go out and purchase your first property. You need some guidance.

Don't worry! You're then offered a one-on-one mentorship program that only costs about $25,000 (at the bottom end). For this fee, you will work one-on-one with a real estate tycoon who will teach you all the tricks of the trade.

Do you see where I'm going with this? By now, you have spent tens of thousands of dollars. You could have used that money for a down payment on a house and already had your first property.

So if you do sign up for a free real estate seminar, do so knowing that their end-game is to upsell you. Don't fall prey to these scams. Real estate investing isn't so difficult that you need to pay someone tens of thousands of dollars to get it right.

You just need a few facts and a little common sense.

How to Earn Passive Income with Real Estate Investing

Let's talk about the right way to do it, shall we?

In order to earn passive income from real estate, you need to have a rental property. You can buy a house, an apartment, condo, duplex, triplex, large multi-family unit, mobile home park, or even a storage unit facility. For our discussion, we'll focus on residential rental properties. And if you're not quite ready to buy a house, I'm going to show you how you can save enough for a down payment in six months.

But first, here are a few facts about the real estate market that may surprise you.

Real Estate Investing Facts You Should Know:

The demand for single family rental homes hit an all-time high last year. Currently, there are 16 million of them, but it's predicted that by 2030, there will be 13 million more on the market.

Most real estate investors strive for $200 per door (unit) net income per month. As you can see from my example, you can do much better if you buy right.

You can scale your rental business and quickly earn tens of thousands per month on rentals.

Depending on the shape of the property and your tenants, you could spend between 1 – 5 hours a month managing it.

Buy and Hold Real Estate

If you want to earn passive income as a real estate investor doing rentals, you will be known as a buy and hold investor. That means you buy properties and hold them. You don't flip them, wholesale them, or do rent-to-own or seller financing deals. You just hold onto them and reap the rewards in rent money, equity build up, and possibly sales proceeds if you decide to sell it down the road.

But when you buy real estate to turn it into a rental, you need to go about it in a methodical and calculating way. If you don't — or if you buy the house based on emotions — it could turn out badly.

For this chapter — and all the other passive income idea chapters in this book — I'm going to walk you step-by-step through the process of becoming a real estate investor specializing in rentals.

In other words, let's go buy a rental house together right now!

Step One: Determine Where You Want to Buy

Your first step in buying a rental house is to determine which area you want to buy in. I'd like to say something here about buying and managing rental properties from a distance.

Although we are about to do that with our beach house, I can't advise it if you're just getting into the rental business. With your first rental house, you should buy a house that's close enough to drive by and see it.

Buying a house is a huge investment, and trusting it to virtual strangers without the opportunity to check on the house every now and then takes nerves of steel. I know people do it, but I'm not going to recommend it.

When tenants know you're nearby, they act differently.

Hiring a property management company is one option that may allow you to buy long-distance rental properties. And while we will talk about that later, I still can't in good conscious recommend managing rentals from afar when you're first starting out.

Let me give you a great example. Recently, the water company called and told me that I had a leak someplace on my property. I checked all the usual places and couldn't find any evidence of a leak, so I called a plumber.

I met him when he arrived, told him about the call and he immediately pulled out a shovel and asked his helper to start digging. He told me it would cost almost $1,000 to dig around the yard and look for the leak.

I refused. Turns out, one of the toilets had a "silent leak" that couldn't be detected by just listening for a leak. The repair cost $150, but could have cost $1,000 or more if I had not been there to personally assess the situation.

When renting properties, you never know what will pop up, and until you get some experience under your belt, it makes sense to be there to personally handle each situation yourself.

That means, at least for your first rental, you should stay close to home.

And if you're going to buy in the city or town you live in, you will need to determine which area of town you want to own in. There are three classes of houses to choose from.

Class A Housing

Class A housing is located in nice neighborhoods where everyone takes care of their homes. The lawns are green, the houses are well-maintained, and they are expensive to buy.

These do not make the best rental investments. The high costs of buying and maintaining them will negatively affect your ability to make a decent cash flow.

Class B Housing

These houses are located in neighborhoods where the working class live. The construction workers, nurses, and blue collar workers live in class B housing, and the neighborhoods are abundant. Most of the people in the neighborhood own their own homes, but around 30 percent of them are rented.

Class B neighborhoods are your sweet spot. Look for rental houses in this type of area.

Class C Housing

When you think about run-down neighborhoods, you're imagining a class C neighborhood. These areas have a higher crime rate, the houses are not well-kept, and most of the people who live there are renters.

While it is possible to earn a decent cash flow from these types of properties, you will work much harder at it. You will likely have more repairs when tenants move out, have a higher turnover rate, and get a lot more calls in the middle of the night.

Some people make a lot of money on these types of rental units, but I don't think buying one as your first rental house is a good idea. Especially if passive income is your goal.

So, your challenge is to find a class B neighborhood in your town or city. Once you do, start looking for a house that peaks your interest.

Most successful rental units are 3 bedrooms with 2 bathrooms, but a lot of that depends on your area.

For instance, my two apartments are both efficiencies and under 400 square feet. But I live in a unique area.

Work with an Agent

If you're not sure what the best type of rental in your area is, call a leasing agent and ask. Tell them you are interested in purchasing rental units and ask what the most popular size rentals are.

Real estate agents have access to deals that may not be public, and that's why most real estate investors develop a relationship with an agent. If you find an agent you think you could work with, tell them what you are looking for and let them find it for you.

Use Online Sites

Another option is to use websites like roofstock to look for investment properties. The homes on this site have been inspected and come with a list of expected repairs. It also provides tenant history, current lease information, and the anticipated return on investment for each property
.
Also, Realtor.com is basically the MLS. You can find the same homes as Realtors (except for-sale-by-owners and other off-market properties) by visiting this site.

Agents can also give you advice about rental rates, and statistics about varying neighborhoods. And since sellers pay Realtor fees, you will get all this knowledge for free.

After you find some properties that meet your guidelines, you'll need to take a couple of preliminary steps before seeing them to determine if they are right for a passive income stream.

2 Steps to Take Before Looking at the Properties in Person

It is critical that you look at rental properties on paper before you ever see them in person. Why? Because it's too easy to fall in love with a house that won't provide you with sufficient passive income — or worse, will cost you money every month.

Once you find some properties that peak your interest, you will need to take two steps to determine whether or not they are good investments.

Determine the Potential Rental Income

Every area has an average price for rentals, and it's important that you know this figure for each of the houses you want to see. You can get this price in a number of way:

- **Ask your Realtor.** He or she may have an idea of what houses rent for in the area. I wouldn't rely on this as your only source of information. My realtor suggested that I rent out my first apartment for $650 when I bought the house, and I rent it for $1,100.
- **Look in the local newspaper and on Craigslist.** Look for houses in the same area and find the ones are similar in square footage as well as the number of bedrooms and bathrooms. Be sure to look at photos so you're comparing similar houses.
- **Use** Rentometer[1]. You can use this site for free for up to five properties. Simply type in the address, and it will give you an estimated rent analysis for the property.

I recommend using a combination of all three methods because none of them are perfect. But if you do your due diligence, you should arrive at a reasonable rent estimate for the properties. (Do this for all the properties you intend to look at.)

The 10 Percent Rule

Your next step is to eliminate the properties that won't offer you the cash flow you need. You will do this by adhering to the 10 percent rule.

---

1. https://www.rentometer.com?afmc=4e&utm_campaign=4e&utm_source=leaddyn o&utm_medium=affiliate

The 10 percent rule is a great way to weed out the houses that won't provide you with enough passive income to make it worth your while — and it will highlight the homes that you should look into further. It's not a formula to identify the *right* rental property, it's a formula to *narrow* down the field.

Remember, you're not buying your family home. You are looking for a house that will provide you with the passive income you need to start building wealth. That's why successful real estate investors don't buy based on emotions — they buy based on the numbers.

Here is the 10 percent rule in a nutshell:

The 10 Percent Rule
You should only look at houses that are 10 percent or higher in this equation. To arrive at this figure, divide your annual projected rental income by the purchase price. For example, imagine the house is priced at $100,000 and you could rent it for $1,000 a month. That makes your annual rental income $12,000 ($1,000 x 12).
To determine whether this house fits the 10 percent rule, divide the annual income ($12,000) by the purchase price ($100,000) to arrive at 12 percent.
This house is worth further consideration.

Now it's Time to See the Property

Now that you have a list of the properties that could turn out to be profitable, it's time to go see them in person and continue the investigation. On your visits, you will need to look for things that will affect your cash flow.

For instance, look at the overall structure of the house to determine what kind of shape the roof in in, look for obvious plumbing leaks, broken fences or decks, outdated flooring, garish paint on the walls, and other things you can see with amateur eyes. Make a list of everything you see.

If the property still interests you, it's time to run some numbers to determine what kind of cash flow you can expect from it.

Here is a simple explanation of cash flow. In a minute, we will get into a more detailed explanation.

What is Cash Flow?

Cash flow is the net amount of money you make every month from the property. To arrive at it, deduct the mortgage payment, property taxes, homeowners insurance, maintenance (such as lawn maintenance), and repairs. The balance is your cash flow.

Here's an example:

Rent = $1,000

Expenses

$475 mortgage

$125 property taxes

$60 homeowner's insurance

$40 maintenance

$100 estimated repairs

Total expenses = $800

Monthly cash flow ($1,000 - $800) = $200

What Do You Count as Expenses?

When looking at a property to determine cash flow, you will need to look at a lot more than the above list. (I just wanted to give you an overview so you would have a mental image of the math before we get into the nitty-gritty.)

Here are the numbers you will need to pay attention to when estimating your cash flow.

Mortgage Payment

Unless you plan to pay cash for the property, you will have a mortgage payment. Look for a fixed 30-year mortgage that allows you to put down as little as possible. You will find all kinds of mortgage payment calculators[2] online that allow you to punch in some numbers and arrive at an estimated payment.

Utilities

Some landlords pay utilities (electric, water, and gas), and you will need to determine if you will. I recommend not doing so unless you have no option. For example, if you purchase a multi-unit property that only has one meter, you have three choices.

- You can split the meters, but this is costly and will reduce your cash flow.
- You can use the RUBS system. With this system, you figure the square footage of each unit and assign that percentage of the utility bills to each renter. This is

---

2. https://www.mortgagecalculator.org/

the system I currently use, although I'm considering changing to the next option.

- You can install meter monitoring devices such as E-mon[3]. These devices measure how much each unit is using. Some devices will email you the stats every month, and then you figure up each tenant's bill and send them an invoice.

If you choose to pay utilities, you will need the numbers to input into your equation. You can get them by calling each of the utility companies (electric, water, and trash) and asking them for a 12-month average. Use that as your monthly expense figure.

Property Taxes

Sometimes, your property taxes are figured into your mortgage payment, but not always. If not, go online to the local county tax assessor and look up the property taxes on the house. Your Realtor can also get this information for you.

Homeowners Insurance

This is also figured in with a mortgage payment by some banks, but not always. You will need to call your insurance agent to determine what your monthly payment will be. I recommend getting a simple fire insurance policy with an umbrella policy giving you additional liability coverage. But be smart and talk to your agent before deciding which type of policy to get.

Trash

---

3. http://pwww.emon.com/en/emon/products

You will also need to determine whether you will be in charge of the monthly garbage fee or your renters. If you plan to pay it, find out what the city charges and figure it in with your expenses.

Homeowners Association Fees (HOAs) and Special Assessments

When you buy a condo, some townhomes, or some upper-end homes you will have monthly HOA fees to pay. I highly advised against buying rental properties that have HOAs. Here's why.

First, the cost of the HOAs can drastically reduce your cash flow. For instance, were I live it's not uncommon for people to pay $500 or more for HOA fees.

Secondly, HOAs come with special assessments. When a homeowners association decides the condo or townhomes need a new roof, a repair to the community swimming pool, or air conditioner units for the entire property, they issue a special assessment that each property owner has to pay. These special assessments can run in the thousands, and paying them isn't an option. People have lost their properties for not being able to afford an unexpected special assessment.

What do you think it would do to your yearly cash flow if your homeowner's association suddenly decided it wanted to put a new roof on the entire complex and came to you for $7,000?

HOAs have their place, but not typically in the real estate rental business.

Property Management Fees

If you don't want to manage your rental property yourself, you can hire a property management company to do it for you. But it will cost you valuable cash flow.

I recommend doing your own property management if you only have a couple of properties, and they are nearby. However, if you buy property in another city or don't want to manage it yourself, you will need to hire a property management company.

These companies typically charge a 10 to 12 percent management fee, and if they have to fill a vacancy, they will charge one-half of a month's rent to a full month's rent for the service.

That means for a property that brings in $1,000 a month in rental income, you would pay a minimum of $100 a month, plus $500 to $1,000 to fill a vacancy each time the property comes available.

Vacancies

Unless you live in a very high-demand area, you will have some vacancies in your rental. And unless you budget for them, you won't meet your financial expectations. Unfortunately, every area's vacancy rates are different so I can't provide you with a figure.

Your best solution is to talk to local investors by attending an investors club. You can find them on local meetups. Then ask them what to expect as far as vacancies. And then figure it into your expenses.

For instance, if the rate around 8 percent, that means your property would be vacant one month of the year. When just starting out, figure a one month vacancy per year is a safe bet.

Maintenance

This one is tricky to figure, but crucial. You will have maintenance on your rental properties, and if you don't figure it into your calculations, you could end up losing money every month.

But those expenses will vary from month to month. For instance, one month you may need to replace the hot water heater and spend $1,500. But the next month, you may only need to fix a broken garbage disposal and spend $125.00. You may not have any expenses for the rest of the year.

Ask the seller for a list of expenditures for the past year, but don't hold your breath for them. Instead, you will probably have to estimate based on what you find when you look at the house. Is it well-kept or does it look like it's been neglected? A good average is about $50 a month or $600 a year. Of course, that could be way off, depending on the shape of the house.

CapEx

Capital improvements and capital expenses go under this column. These are things that are major improvements to the house. Some examples of CapEx expenses are replacing the roof, rewiring the house, installing a new septic system, installing a new air conditioner, adding on to the house, or repaving the driveway. They are expenses that must be done, but aren't considered repairs because they add value to the house.

You will have CapEx expenses, and the key is to budget for them to avoid them coming as a surprise. After all, you will have renters in the home. What would happen if the air conditioner went out, but you didn't have the funds to replace it?

That's where budgeting for these expenses comes in. I recommend budging 7 percent of your gross rents for these expenses. In other words, if your rent is $1,000 a month, $70 of it goes into a CapEx account in case of a major expense.

Putting it all Together

Once you have your numbers, it's time to add them all up and determine how the house will cash flow. I'll give you an example below to give you a visual.

Example Cash Flow Projections

Price of house: $100,000
Gross rent: $1,000

Expenses:
Mortgage $450
Property tax $100
Homeowners insurance $50
Insurance $60
Utilities $0
Trash $0
Property management $0
Maintenance $50
CapEx $70
Total Expenses $780.00

Rent ($1,000) – Expenses ($780.00) =
$220

The above example is cutting it pretty close to the $200 minimum per unit goal that we set. Can you see how paying tenant's utilities or add a property management company to the mix can affect your bottom line?

A Word About Renovations

Many times, when you buy a rental house it will need some renovations. It may need new floors, appliances, or an added bathroom. Before you hire the contractors, you should take the following steps.

Get Bids

It's important to know what it will cost to do the renovations you want. Get at least three bids from contractors.

Calculate your Return on Investment (ROI)

In order to determine whether or not you should do the renovations, you need to know how long they will take to pay for themselves. Here's how to figure it:

Take your contractor's bid and add 10 percent. (Trust me). Then, divide that number by your monthly rent. That's how long it will take you to recoup your investment. Here's how it looks:

New floors $4,800. Monthly rent $1,000 ($4,800 / $1,000 = 4.8 months.)

The general rule of thumb is that if a minor repair like flooring pays for itself within 2 years, it's a solid investment. And if a larger repair like a roof or new air conditioners pays for itself within 6 years, it's probably worthwhile.

Keep in mind that every time you do repairs on your house, you may be able to increase the rent when new renters move in.

How to Finance a Rental Property

Despite what you hear on the infomercials, financing a rental property can be tough—but not impossible. You may have to engage in a little creative financing to get the deal done, but hey, that's what real estate investors do.

Before we get into how to find financing, there are a few things you should know about when you're applying for a rental loan with a lender:

- Most lenders will only give up to four loans to an investor. The government guidelines state that they can give you ten, but you will have to work hard to find one that will do it.
- Don't work with mortgage brokers when trying to buy a rental investment house. It's a completely different game that they don't understand. Your best bet is to work with a direct lender. (More about this later)
- You need a sizable down payment if you're going to get a loan. For loans one through four, you will need 20 percent down, and for loans five through ten, you'll need to put down 25 percent. There are other options and we'll talk about those, too.
- The lender will also require that you have six months

of cash reserves in the bank when buying a rental property. That means six months of mortgage payments (for both houses if you already own one), and other debt.

- Your credit matters. For your first through your fourth loan, you need at least a 630 credit rating. For loans five through ten, you need a 720.
- The lender will want to see two years of solid earnings. For those who work for others, you will need to show W-2 tax returns for the past two years, and the lender will average them. For the self-employed, be prepared to show two years of tax returns, a profit and loss statement, and a certified letter from your CPA stating that your records are correct.

Here are some of the most methods investors use to finance rental properties.

Go to Your Local Lender

Your loan savings and loan or credit union is a great place to start when looking for a rental property loan. But know that they will require most of the things I listed above. Lenders consider rental property loans riskier than traditional housing loans, so they ask for more from their borrowers.

Online Lenders

Online lenders are another great way to apply for a rental property loan. With sites like Rocket Mortgage, LoanDepot, Lending Tree, and Quicken Loans, you can input your information and get a credit decision back quickly.

Applying for a mortgage online will save you time because after inputting your information from home, you can compare your offers at your convenience and choose the one that offers you the best deal.

Seller financing

If you can't qualify for a mortgage, all is not lost. Some sellers will finance the house for. In fact, this is how I bought my first house. The seller should own the house clear and free, and they can carry the note for you just like a bank would.

Seller financing deals are common, but if you want to buy your first rental investment property this way, you will have to approach the seller professionally. Here are some hints to find and secure seller financing.

- Look online for seller financing deals. For instance, on Realtor.com you can set the filter to look for sellers who offer financing.
- Tell your Realtor you are looking for seller financing deals.
- Look at houses that are for sale by owner. A lot of these sellers are open to financing the deal themselves.

Seller financing deals should be done just like any other deal. The seller will give you a deed of trust on the property, and you will sign loan papers. It's wise to include an attorney in these deals to make sure everyone is legally protected.

Wrap Notes

A wraparound mortgage is a relatively new way of buying a house, but it's not legal in all states so be sure to check with yours before trying to make this kind of deal. Here's how it works: a seller has a mortgage on their house, but the need to sell it. You want to buy the house, but you can't quality for a mortgage.

So, you agree to give the seller a small down payment, maybe 10 percent, and then take over the mortgage payments. The seller then has a second lien on the property. This type of loan is tricky because in most mortgage agreements, the seller has the right to call the loan due if the house is sold. Apparently, mortgage holders don't typically do this, but if they wanted to, they could.

Wrap mortgages are very common in some states such as Texas, but I urge caution on them. Have a note called due is a pretty big risk to take.

Partner with an Investor

If you want to make a rental property purchase but don't have any money, you can also partner with an investor who does. You meet these investors at the local real estate clubs. Many people have entered the real estate investing market this way. The investor provides the money, and you find the deal and manage the property. You remain partners, splitting the profits until the house is sold. And then you split those profits.

If you're going to approach one of these investors, be smart about it. Go in prepared with all of your facts and numbers laid out in an easy-to-understand format.

Home Equity Loans and Home Equity Lines of Credit

If you already own a home and have some equity in it, you may be able to qualify for a home equity loan (HEL) or a home equity line of credit (HELOC). Both types of loan advance loans on the equity in your home, usually about 65 percent of the equity.

This is an excellent way to get enough money for a down payment on your rental property, or if you have enough equity, to pay cash for it. But keep in mind that if something goes wrong and you can't pay the note, it will put your primary residence at risk.

Hard Money Loans

Private lenders give these types of loans, and although they are easier to get because the lender cares about the asset rather than your finances, they come at a price. You will pay much higher interest rates for a private money loan, and the loan period will be for a shorter amount of time.

Hard money loans are meant to be for the short term. People use them to flip houses or as a temporary loan until they can secure another loan. I don't recommend anyone but the most experienced investor use these loans.

What Not to Do

Did you notice that I didn't mention credit cards or private loans? While it is possible to get a cash advance on your credit card or take out a 24-month private loan for a down payment, it's not advisable.

Here's why: Let's imagine you need a $20,000 down payment for the $100,000 rental property you want to buy. To get a cash advance, you will pay the credit card company 3 to 4 percent for the privilege. And then pay 20-something percent interest on top of that.

And personal loans are no better. These short-term loan payment are high enough to knock your cash flow into the negative.

What if You Don't Have any Money?

So, what do you do if you are ready to invest in rental properties, but don't have the money for a down payment and can't find a seller who is willing to finance your deal?

Start saving.

If you have good credit and can quality for a traditional mortgage, all you need as a down payment on a $100,000 rental property is about $3,500 (3.5 percent). While that sounds like a lot of money, the truth is you can save it faster than you think.

Start by renting a room in your house. It can be a spare bedroom, a guest house, or even rent your garage as a storage unit.

When you collect the rent every month, sock it away into your rental property fund.

Then cut back on expenses and put every penny you save into the rental house fund.

Have a garage sale, sell stuff on eBay, start a side gig, or get a second job.

Do a Dave Ramsey and save like nobody's business. Trust me, if you put your mind to it, it will be easier than you imagine.

Here's an idea of what it looks like.

How to Save $3,500 Fast

1. Have a garage sale ($250)
2. Rent a spare bedroom for 6 months (6 x $500 = $3,000)
3. Eat at home for 6 months and conserve on your grocery bill $250

Total: $3,500

Management Tips

Once you purchase your first rental property, you will need to manage it in a way that involves the least amount of work. After all, you wanted it as a form of passive income, didn't you?

Here are some tips and tricks that will help you manage your property right.

- **Use Cozy[4] or another landlord website.** These sites allow you to take applications online, screen applicants from the comfort of your home, and collect rent remotely. It will be deposited in your account automatically every month. For the passive income landlord, it just doesn't get any easier than this.
- **Hire a professional** to take photos of your unfurnished rental, and then make them even more wonderful by using Box Brownie[5] virtual staging to insert virtual furniture. This company will make your rental look like a professionally designed space and give renters ideas about how to place their furniture. I only recommend using this $32 per room feature if you have trouble attracting renters.
- **Use a month-to-month lease.** I would never sign a long-term lease with my tenants because a month-to-month lease prevents too many problems. For example, my renter who tried to sell drugs from my

---

4. **https://cozy.co/**

5. https://www.boxbrownie.com/virtual-staging

apartment was out in a week because we had a
month-to-month lease. If he had signed a year-long
lease, I would have had to start costly eviction
proceedings that could have dragged on for months.
A month-to-month lease doesn't mean you're only
renting the space short-term. My tenants stay long-
term, but if either of us have a change of heart, we can
give a 30-day written notice to end the lease. It's
important to check your state laws, but for most, a
month-to-month lease will better protect your
interests.

- **Keep security deposits separate.** When a tenant
  moves out, you will have about 30-days to return
  their security deposit, minus any expenses you're out
  for repairing damage they caused. You should keep
  tenant's security deposits in a separate bank account.
  Remember, it's their money, not yours, and in some
  states failure to keep it separate and available can
  result in steep fines.

- **Carefully consider pet policies.** Renters with pets
  have a difficult time finding properties that will
  accept them. Personally, I allow small pets in my
  units, but with strict rules. The pets must be on leases
  when in shared space, and no barking dogs are
  allowed. You can charge a monthly fee for pets or a
  non-refundable pet deposit.

- **Require renter's insurance.** Renter's insurance will
  protect your renters in case of a break in or other
  mishap, but it can also protect you. If they cause
  damage over and above their security deposit, you

can work with their insurance company to collect.

- **Use smart locks.** If you want to be as passive as possible, install smart locks on your units and use them to show the property when looking for tenants. You can change the codes as often as you want, but if you don't want to show every potential tenant the space, simply give them the code and ask them to contact you if they're interested.

- **Stay in contact**. Ask tenants to let you know as soon as a problem crops up, and then get it repaired right away. That will go a long way in preventing costly repairs.

- **Enforce your late fee**. When signing the lease, let tenants know that you are serious about on-time rent, and the late fee applies the day after the rent is due. Don't accept late rent without the late fees attached. This will ensure they pay on time from then on.

What Kind of Passive Income Can You Expect From Rentals?

Now that you understand the wonderful world of real estate, what do you think? Can you imagine building wealth by buying one rental property at a time? You will not only create cash flow, but you will build a portfolio of properties that increase in value every year.

But you won't pay for it.

I'm convinced that real estate rentals are the best way to build passive income, and that's why I started with this income stream idea.

Rental Properties Help Lower Your Tax Rate

Another great benefit of owning rental properties is the tax savings. When you rent out your property, the IRS allows you to depreciate the house (not the property) over 27.5 years. That's a huge tax savings. Here's an example:

Your house is appraised at $300,000. (House only, remember you can't depreciate the land).
Your yearly tax write off for the next 27.5 years is $10,909. ($300,000 / 27.5)

Talk about passive income!

But there's more. Follow along in the next chapter as we talk about how to create passive income streams with rentals of a different kind.

Chapter Seven: Leverage Your Belongings for Passive Income

So far, I've drilled it into your head that in order to earn passive income, you have to do some upfront work. And while the income streams I'm about to present to you do take a tiny amount of work, they don't take much.

I'm talking about using what you already own to create streams of income.

Sound too good to be true? I assure you, it's not.

Here's how it works: the sharing economy opened up a lot of possibilities for people who want to earn extra income. For instance, you can drive an Uber or deliver food to people who don't want to get it themselves.

But that's not exactly passive is it?

But did you know that the sharing economy has created a lot of way to earn passive income simply by renting out the things you already own? It's true.

So, in this chapter, I'm going to outline a lot of ways you can leverage the things you already own and rent them out to create some forms of passive income.

Will it make you as wealthy as real estate rentals? No. But it will provide you with steady streams of income that you can use to pay bills — or to save up for that first rental property.

Here we go — here are the best ways to earn passive income from the sharing economy.

Rent a Spare Bedroom

We touched on this a little bit in the last chapter, but now I want to talk to you about your options and give you some concrete steps to begin earning passive income this way.

You have two options when it comes to renting out a spare bedroom in your home.

- Rent it to a long-term renter who will stay for a while (Long-term rentals)
- Rent it to people who only want to stay for short periods of time (Short-term rentals)

Let's start with how to rent out your spare bedroom long-term.

How to Use Your Spare Bedroom for Long-Term Rental Income

There are many people who want to rent a place to live, but they don't want to pay the exorbitant amounts charged by apartment complexes and landlords these days. Let's be real: rents have skyrocketed in the past few years, and that has left a lot of people looking for options.

That's why so many people look for rooms to rent instead of entire houses or apartments. And if you have a spare bedroom in your home (or even more than one), you can start earning some cash flow.

But you will need to take some carefully planned steps to rent out a room in your home successfully. Here is what the process looks like.

Decide What You Will Charge

Your first step in the process is to decide what you will charge. I put this first because if you determine that renting out a room isn't worth it to you, then you won't have wasted a lot of time.

To determine what you could your room for, look on Craigslist. There, you will find other room rentals in your area with photos. Look at the photos and the rent price, and then use them to come up with a fair rental price for your room.

For instance, if moderately nice rooms in your area rent for $500 a month, you can comfortably set your rent at that price. And if the room has a private bathroom, you will likely get more for it.

You also need to decide how to handle the utilities such as electric, water, and trash. Since both of you will be using the utilities, you can split them, or ask the renter to contribute a set amount every month.

Some people offer free utilities, but I recommend against that. After all, if you are opening up your home to strangers to earn passive income, you should try to earn as much as possible. Plus, it's just common sense that if someone isn't paying for utilities, they're not going to make an effort to conserve. And if your electric or gas bill goes up, that cuts into your profit.

Once you determine your price, decide whether the amount is worth having a stranger live in your home. Some people are comfortable with this, while others aren't, so be sure to think hard about your decision.

Rental Income is Taxable
Don't forget to pay taxes on the income you make from renting out a spare room. But along with the tax burden comes the benefit of getting to deduct the expenses related to your rental activities.

Get Your House Ready

If you decide to go ahead, your next step is to get your house ready. You can no longer leave valuable items lying around the house, and you should fix anything that is broken. For example, put your expensive jewelry in a safe, or take that cash out from under your mattress and put it in the bank.

And if things are broken that the renter would use — such as the microwave or shower handle — fix them before renting the house.

Also clean up both the interior and exterior of your home. Clean the inside thoroughly and organize the kitchen so it will be comfortable for your renter. Take out old food from the fridge and pantry and organize it so they will have room for their food, too.

Then move on to the outside of your home. Cut the grass, weed the beds, and haul off any garbage you have lying around. Plant some pretty flowers in pots. Curb appeal not only applies to home buyers but home renters as well.

Finally, you need to address the locks on the doors. To avoid getting locked out of your own home, you should replace all interior and exterior locks with smart locks. These locks make it easy for you to change the code when necessary, and it will make it impossible for anyone to lock you out of the spare bedroom or your home.

Decide Which Rooms to Rent

The nicer the room the more money you will collect in rent. You can choose to rent out the spare bedroom — or bedrooms if you have more than one — or you can move into a spare bedroom and rent out the master with a private bath for more money. You can also rent out a converted basement or attic as long as it's build to code.

Add to Your Insurance Policy

If you plan to rent out your room for six months or longer, you will need to add a landlord policy to your homeowner's insurance policy. Talk to you agent about the specifics.

Run an Ad

Now it's take to let the world know you have a room for rent. You should run an ad in the local paper, on Craigslist, and other places the people in your local community look for houses such as Facebook groups.

Don't try to please everyone when running your ad by making your room sound like an oasis. Your goal in getting people to respond is to get the *right* people interested in your room.

If you can't stand the smell of cigarette smoke, state in the ad that you won't rent to smokers. If you're quiet, make it clear that loud parties or a bunch of guests aren't welcome in the house. If you keep a strict schedule of going to bed early at night and waking up early, your renter will ideally follow that same type of schedule. Otherwise, the arrangement can quickly become uncomfortable.

Set up Interviews

Now that you've received some interest from the ad, it's time to meet some of your potential roommates. This part of the process can be tricky because people tend to put their best foot forward when first meeting someone. But by asking specific questions, you can weed out potential problems.

And notice I indicated that you would be the one asking questions. You don't want to give too much away on your first interviews because you don't know the people. For instance, you don't want them to know your routine, what valuables are in your home, or the fact that you are all alone and don't have any family nearby.

Instead, use the interview to talk about the house, what you are offering, and ask them questions. Here are some questions you should ask:

- Why type of job do you have?

- What does your daily schedule look like?
- Do you have a significant other who stays over at your place?
- Do you have pets?
- What do you like to do in the evening?
- Do you cook at home often?
- Are you a neat person?
- What do you do on weekends?
- How much stuff do you have?
- Do you smoke?
- Drink?

You get the picture. Your job during the interview process is to ask them enough questions to determine whether living in the same house as them is feasible.

Ask each person that you interview the same types of questions, and be sure to keep good notes.

After the first round, narrow down your choices and ask the finalists back for a second interview. This is where you should determine whether or not their personality is a good fit for your home.

In addition, this is where you should ask for proof of their job or school. For instance, if they say they work at the local plant, ask to see their last paystub. And if they claim to be a college student, ask to see their student ID.

You need to make sure they are who they say they are before agreeing to rent space to them.

Run Credit and Background Checks

Once you've found the tenant you like, it's time to run a credit report and background check on them. After all, you're allowing a stranger to move into your home — shouldn't you first make sure they can pay the rent and don't have a criminal history?

In the past, landlords were forced to run a hard credit check on tenants, a practice that can hurt a renter's credit score. But now with companies like Cozy[1], you can ask the tenant to pull their own credit report, which results in a soft credit check. And that won't hurt their credit.

The same is true for a background check. Cozy will allow the tenant to order their background check and then share it with you.

Ask them to Sign the Lease and Rental Rules Contract

Once you've found the right tenant it's time to make it official. Your first order of business is to draw up a lease (month-to-month), and ask them to sign it. You can find free templates on the internet, but because each state's rental laws are different, I recommend finding one approved by your state. When they sign, ask them for the first and last month's rent and the security deposit.

Next, draw up a separate rules sheet that outlines the rules of the house. For example, no loud noise after 10 pm, no perma-

1. https://cozy.co/for-landlords/tenant-screening/

nent roommates, or a requirement to clean the kitchen after every meal.

These rules will help keep your sanity, and if broken, they will give you a reason to end the month-to-month lease.

Congratulations, you now have a passive income stream that not only gives you money every month, but also helps lower your utilities.

But wait, what if you don't want someone else living in your house full-time? Don't worry, it's possible to create a passive income stream by only renting out your spare bedroom on a part-time basis.

How to Use Your Spare Bedroom for Short-Term Rental Income

Surely, you've heard of Airbnb[2], HomeAway[3], and VRBO[4], but did you know that ordinary people just like you are using them to create semi-passive income streams? It's true. Depending on where you live, you can rack in thousands of dollars per month by renting out your spare bedroom for short-term stays.

Let's take a look at this semi-passive income stream and see if it's right for you.

Set a Price

---

2. https://www.airbnb.com/

3. https://www.homeaway.com/

4. https://www.vrbo.com/

When renting long-term, you set a monthly price but when renting out your room part time, you will charge guests for each night they spend in your home. There are numerous ways to come up with the price, but these two are the most sensible.

Look at the Competition

Log onto one of the short-term rental places I mentioned above and do some digging. Set the parameters and look for available rooms in your area by selecting the number of guests (how many people can comfortably fit in the space), the size of the space, and whether it is an entire house, an apartment or condo, or one room.

Once you've found similar rooms for rent, make a list of their prices. Be sure to pay close attention to the room's décor and amenities so you're comparing apples to apples. For instance, if you will offer a shared bathroom, don't compare your rental to one that offers a private bathroom.

By looking at all the competition, you should be able to come up with a competitive price. Next, look on the calendars of your competitors. Each one will show you which nights are booked, and that will give you an idea of how many nights you can expect people to book your room.

Use Pricing Software

Your other option for finding the right price for your short-term rental is to go to AirDNA[5]. This app will analyze your property, compare it to others in your area, and give you an

---

5. https://www.airdna.co/

estimate of what you should charge. (You can run a couple of searches for free, but if you want to use it more, you will have to sign up and pay a small fee)

Once you determine the price you can charge per night, multiply it by the average number of nights your competitors are booked. For example, if your competitors charge $75 a night, and are booked 20 nights out of a month, you can reasonably expect to earn $1,500 a month less expenses and fees.

Do you now understand why so many people use short-term rentals as a semi-passive income stream? (We'll get to why this is semi-passive in a moment.)

Get Your Room Ready

Short-term renters are a different breed, and you will have to make your home ready for them in an entirely new way. Think of your room as a hotel room — what do you expect to have when you check in?

Many Airbnb owners provide luxury mattresses, nice linens, clean towels, shampoo and conditioner, coffee pots, snacks, cold water bottles in the mini-fridge, smart key access, pots, pans, and other kitchen necessities, DVD players, cable, WIFI, and anything else people need to enjoy a nice, clean, comfortable stay.

You can find plenty of YouTube videos that talk about how to make ready a room for a successful short-term stay. Tricks like folding towels, typing ribbons around them and placing them in a basket are popular. And some hosts go as far as to welcome their guests with freshly baked goods or a bottle of wine.

You should look for your signature "gift" to leave in the room for every rental. Guests will notice, and it may result in good reviews—the lifeblood of your short-term rental business.

Here are the steps you need to take if you're serious about renting our room or house to short-term renters.

Check Your Local Zoning Laws

Not all areas allow people to rent out their houses or rooms for the short-term. Even the beach town I live in only allows certain areas of the town to be used for short-term rentals.

And since Airbnb has taken over the short-term stay market, many cities are passing laws prohibiting or limiting the practice. So be sure to check your town to make sure you can rent your room this way.

Up Your Insurance

If you rent your room to short-term guests, your regular homeowner's policy won't cover any damages they do to your house or any liabilities that come from accidents. To play it safe, talk to your insurance agent and ask to add a rider or endorsement to your homeowner's policy.

Know Your Local Laws

Many municipalities have created new laws and policies for people who rent short-term. For instance, some cities require inspections of the property before you can rent it, others charge for permits, and still others impose licensing fees and taxes on hosts.

Be sure to check with your town or city to find out what you need to do to make your rental legal.

List Your Property

Now that you've prepared your room, it's time to list it. To have a successful listing, you will need to do the following:

- Have a creative title that speaks to your target audience. For example, your target guest might be older couples looking for a quiet evening in a comfortable bed, or a businessman who wants easy access to downtown.
- A description of your room that makes people want to stay. Highlight the features of your room so that people can imagine themselves staying there. Also, be sure to highlight the amenities. Does the house have a pool, a nearby park, or is it walking distance to the downtown area?
- Include professionally shot photos of the room. Don't try to take the photos yourself — there is just too much competition. Your room should look "Instagram-worthy," and only a pro can accomplish that.
- A great host profile. Tell them a little about yourself.
- Excellent reviews. Travelers who use Airbnb rely on reviews to decide whether or not to book a room.

Work hard to get great reviews on your page.

Automate Your System

Remember I said short-term rentals are only semi-passive income? Let me tell you why. You have two choices when it comes to short-term rentals: you can do everything yourself, or you can hire a management team to do it for you.

In other words, short-term rentals are as passive as you want them to be — but you must set them up according to how much time you want to put into them.

Here are some of the things you (or your property management company) need to do to keep your listing operating at peak level:

- Clean after every guest
- Stay on top of your pricing and adjust it if the market conditions require it
- Order new supplies as you need them
- Interact with guests to answer questions

That doesn't sound very passive, does it? But it can be.

Here's my recommendation: for your first short-term rental, do everything yourself. It will teach you what it takes to do each job — and a business person needs to understand their model.

After you're comfortable with it, hire a management company to do it for you. Sure, you will pay fees, but if your goal is passive income, you have to hand the ball to someone else.

But wait, not everyone has an extra bedroom or basement they can use to generate passive income from short-term rentals! That's okay, because it's not the only part of your house that you can rent out to create passive income.

Let's talk about another often forgotten income-generating space.

Rent Out Your Garage

If you have a garage, you could easily begin making (very) passive income every month by renting it out. Storage facilities are popping up all over the country as people accumulate more and more stuff that they don't have room for.

But those storage facilities are expensive and are oftentimes located in areas that are inconvenient for most people. The solution for many people is to rent a private garage.

Landlords have been renting their garages separately for years, but the general public is just learning about this great passive income stream.

Here is what you need to do to get your garage ready to rent.

Determine Your Price

Again, your first step is to determine the price you could get for renting your garage. That's because you want to ensure it's well worth the effort. And prices will vary depending on where you live. In some cities, you can ask $350 for a garage, while others may only bring in $150 a month. To put that in perspective, that's $1,800 to $4,200 a year for doing absolutely nothing.

If you don't have a garage, but do have a parking space in the driveway, a carport, or an area perfect for parking RVs or boats, you can rent out those areas as well.

The best way to determine your price is to look on Craigslist and see what others in your area are renting their garages for.

Clean it Out

If you're going to rent your garage, it needs to be a clean slate. That means hauling off all that stuff you never use or transferring it someplace else. And if you have a garage door opener, you should ensure that it works well.

When you're done, the garage should look clean and empty.

Be sure to take photos of it so you can include them when you advertise it for rent.

Advertise It

Next, you need to let people know that your garage is for rent. You can advertise it on Craigslist, in your local paper or Facebook group, Hopperstock[6], or on STOWIT[7], a website specifically designed to help people rent their garages.

Rent It

When someone wants to rent the garage, you should sign a month-to-month lease for it just as you would an apartment or room.

---

6. https://hopperstock.com/

7. https://www.stowit.com/

And if the new renter asks for a discount, you should consider offering them 10 percent off of your listed price if they pay for the garage a year in advance.

When renting your garage, you will need to include some specifics in your rental agreement:

- State that the garage cannot be used as a repair shop
- The agreement should prohibit anyone from living in the garage
- The renter should carry insurance for contents. For example, if they store a classic car and the roof falls in, you don't want to be responsible.
- You will need to determine how the renter will pay for the electric they use. You might include a flat fee to pay for it if it's not on a separate meter.

As you can see, renting your garage — or parking space, carport or concrete slab — is a great way to earn passive income. Just think, if you can only get the bottom rate for your garage, that's $1,800 a year you did not have to work for!

Rent Your Car

While we're on the subject of garages, let's talk about another way to rent your stuff for passive income. Turo[8] is a car rental website that turned normal car rentals on its head. With Turo, you can rent your car to people who need a car for a day, or people who are visiting town and don't want to use a typical car rental.

---

8. https://turo.com/list-your-car

This works for cars, minivans, trucks, motorcycles, or any other vehicle that you own. And here's the deal: you can scale this passive income business to make more money.

Here's how you do it:

Analyze Your Car

You have to have a decent car to make passive income by renting it. But there are exceptions to this rule. For example, if you have an old pickup truck, someone may not care what it looks like—they only want to rent a truck to haul things.

But if you're going to rent a car, it should be clean, in good working order, and have some current features.

Check the competition

Next, you need to decide whether or not it's worth it for you rent your car. Go to Truo, and look for cars similar to yours in your city. Try to find the same model and year, and then compare the prices.

Next, look on the calendar for that car to see how many days it's rented.

Then multiply the car rental price times the days rented and you'll get your gross profit. For example, if you have a 2012 sedan that could rent for $50 a day, and people with similar cars rent them 22 days a month, you could expect $1,100 in gross profits.

But wait, you don't get to keep all of that.

Turo charges a 25 percent commission for every rental, which leaves you with $825.00 ($1,100 - $275 = $825.00)

To get a true picture of your net profit, you should deduct your car payment and car insurance from your gross profit. Let's say your car payment is $175 and your car insurance is $50 a month. That totals $225 a month.

Now deduct that from $825, and your total profit for the month is $600.00 ($825 - $225 = $600)

Are you seeing what I'm seeing? You will not only earn $600 a month in passive income, but your car payment and insurance will be paid by the people who rent your car.

Let's explore this awesome passive income opportunity further and learn exactly how to do it.

List Your Car

Your first step in the process is to go to Turo.com and list your car. It's an easy signup process and takes about ten minutes.

When listing your car, here are a few things to remember:

- **Use the description area to sell.** Don't just tell readers the model and year of your car. They will see hundreds of listing in your area, and you need to make yours stand out. Highlight any features about your car such as a luggage rack, GPS system, great speakers, or a trailer hitch.
- **Choose the location wisely.** Because you will be using Turo as a passive income stream, you won't

offer to drop off and pick up the car. For instance, many people meet the car renters at the airport when they arrive and then pick up the car when they leave. But since you won't do that, your location will make or break the deal for many people. The closer you are to the airport or downtown the better. But if you're not located there, just use your address for the pickup and drop off location to ensure this remains a passive income stream.

- **Don't use Turo's automatic pricing feature.** This won't allow you to be competitive. Price your car manually, and then change it when your competitors lower or raise their prices. To get the maximum number of bookings, you should always be the lowest price unless your car has a feature that others don't. And be sure to raise your rental rates on holidays and weekends to maximize your profits.

- **Mind your calendar.** You should black out any days on your calendar that you don't want to rent the car, and it will show as unavailable. But remember, the more days you rent it, the higher your profits will be.

- **Set book times.** You have the option of setting a minimum advanced notice requirement. This allows you set the minimum amount of time that renters have to book in advance. You can set it for an hour or a day—it entirely depends on your schedule.

- **Set length limitations**. You can also decide whether you will rent your car for only short-term trips, such as a day or two, or long terms. Some people want to rent a car for a month, and you can add your preferences on your dashboard.

- **Set mileage limitations.** Finally, you should set your mileage restrictions. When someone rents your car, they will only be able to drive it for the amount of miles you set, or Turo will bill them for .75 cents for each mile they go over. Many people on Turo set their restrictions to "unlimited miles."

Scale Up

If you can clear $600 a month on one car (Okay, you will have to clean the car after each rental—or if you want pure passive income, you can pay someone to do it for you), then how much could you earn if you scaled up and offered more cars?

It all depends on your area and the amount of rentals you can expect from it. If you live in an area where Turo is hot, you may be able to keep multiple cars rented out most days of the month. That could easily translate into thousands of dollars a month from passive income.

Some people talk about leasing a car for a low monthly payment and then renting it out on Turo until all of the allowed lease miles are used up, but I caution you against this. First of all, it's against Turo's terms of service to lease a leased car. And if you do and the renter wrecks the car, you could have some serious issues.

But what if you bought additional cars for low monthly payments and leased them? It's entirely doable, but if you decide to go this route, I would advise that you do the following:

- Don't buy a second car until you have a solid track record with your first car. You can only make this decision based on knowledge from your experience, not on guesses about what you could earn.
- Before you buy another car, have it checked out mechanically. You don't want your renters to have to deal with a broken down car.
- If you have a good track record with your first car, think about buying a similar car because you know people will rent it. If you can't find the same model, check the Turo listings before you buy to determine which cars are rented the most.

What About Insurance?

One of the biggest questions people have when thinking about renting their car on Turo is what happens if someone wrecks your car?

And that's a great question.

Turo of course has thought about that. They offer owners three policies: basic, standard, and premium. These policies vary, but the gist of it is that if a renter damages your car, Turo's insurance will pay for it.

In addition, you will get $1 million in liability protection from all three of their plans.

They offer coverage up to $125,000. They use third-party appraisers to determine your car's worth after a wreck, and then it pays 20 percent of the first $3,750 in repairs, and 100 percent after that.

Buyers will also have the option of purchasing a Turo insurance plan just like they do when they rent a car from a national chain, but they are not required to.

Are You Excited About Passive Income?

If your car is just sitting around the driveway and costing you money, renting it out may be a great way to bring in some extra cash.

But Wait, There's More

Just think, depending on where you live, you could rent out your spare bedroom, garage, and car on the days you don't use it and bring in hundreds — if not thousands — of passive income dollars.

Are you ready to learn how to rent out the other stuff you probably already own?

Rent Your Stuff

As if we haven't talked enough about how to turn your possessions into passive income, I've got one more tidbit for you.

It's possible to earn income from all that stuff you have laying around the house and never use.

I'm talking about Fat Llama[9], a site where people go to rent things they need but don't have. For example, someone may

9. https://fatllama.com/

need to rent a camera for a weekend trip, a lawnmower because they're just broke down, a projector to watch old films, a drone, bicycle, musical instruments, a wedding dress, or even a skateboard.

People are earning thousands of dollars a month from this site, but to earn that much, you need to have stuff that people want to rent. I suggest visiting the website and browsing the listing. You'll quickly find that you can literally rent anything that is in good condition and useful.

Here's how to earn passive income using this site:

- List your items. It doesn't cost anything to list your items for rent and it only takes a few minutes. Be sure to include a photo in your listing.
- When someone contacts you, arrange for pickup for delivery of the item. If you're doing this for passive income, you should ask the person to pick up the item to reduce your workload.
- The renter pays through the site and you will be paid three days after the item is returned.

And that's it. If you have a garage full of lawn equipment, sports equipment, kitchen appliances, photography equipment, or anything else that people need, you can easily earn passive income by listing it on this site.

Rent Your Car—In a Different Way

If you don't want to rent your car to other people, think about renting it to a company. And you won't even have to hand them the keys.

Here's what I'm talking about: you can agree to have your wrapped in a way that advertises a company, and then get paid for driving it. That's it. And according to Wrapify[10], the app that makes this possible, drivers average $400 to $600 a month, just for driving your car as you normally would.

Talk about passive income!

Here's how it works:

- You choose between a lite, partial, or full wrap. The more you wrap your car, the more passive income you will earn.
- You deliver your car and when you pick it up, it will be wrapped.
- You drive about 100 minutes a day—what most do anyway.
- You are paid for every mile you drive.

That's it-seriously. You could literally earn enough to pay off your car just by driving it as you normally would.

10. http://www.wrapify.com/

Chapter Eight: Write Your Way to Passive Income

More than 1,600 people search for the term "How to publish a book" on Google every single hour.

That's a lot of people who think writing books is a great way to earn passive income. And since this type of income stream makes up a large part of mine, I feel the need to include it in this book.

But be warned, many people will tell you that publishing books isn't passive income.

But I disagree. Big time.

While it's true that you have to write the book and occasionally market it, it falls into the same group as real estate rentals. You have to do the work upfront, and then you can sit back and reap the rewards.

For years.

For example, I published my first book three years ago, and I still receive income from it. I update the book once a year, which takes about 5 hours, and I run an ad for it maybe once a year.

Total time invested each year: 5 hours and 10 minutes.

And the checks continue to come in every month.

If that's not passive income, I don't know what is.

So, was it passive when I wrote the book? No.

Is it passive now? Oh yeah.

How to Write Books and Earn Passive Income

Before I start this chapter, I need to tell you that I cannot cover the entire topic in a single chapter. I wrote an entire book[1] on the subject, and believe me, it's a complex topic that you need to thoroughly understand before you decide whether or not this is the right passive income stream for you.

But what I can do is give you a brief overview of the topic and talk to you about how you can use book publishing as a fantastic passive income stream.

Before we start, I need to make something clear. Not everyone who publishes a book goes on to earn passive income. In fact, many first-time authors only make about $100 on their book.

But it doesn't have to be that way.

Publishing books, just as any other business, has to be approached seriously. I often see books listed on Amazon that were published a couple of years ago, and they don't even have their first review. The authors of those book obviously aren't involved in making them a success.

But if you're willing to put in the upfront work, it is very possible to earn a great passive income stream from books.

---

1. https://goo.gl/jYSZlH

Again, I can't deal in specifics here — I spent 150 pages doing that in my other book—but I can give you enough basics to know whether this is a passive income stream you want to pursue.

Let's talk about the upfront work you have to do to produce a book, and then we'll talk about joy of receiving royalty checks every month after that.

But first, I have a question for you.

Can You Write?

It's a silly question, I know. But you would be surprised at the number of people who publish books that are barely readable. Unless you can write a book that people want to read, it isn't possible to earn a decent living at it.

After all, for a book to be successful, it has to express an idea or plot that readers want to follow. A non-fiction book should teach readers something they didn't know before they picked up the book. And a fiction book should entertain readers enough that they don't want to put it down.

That's the number one factor in whether or not you can earn passive income from publishing books.

What if I Can't Write?

Maybe you've always dreamed of publishing books, but don't have the skill to write one. In that case, you have two choices.

Hire a Ghostwriter

Some publishers hire other writers to write books for them, and then they publish them under their name. But this can be tricky. In order to be successful, you will have to find a great writer who doesn't charge a fortune to write a good book. And they will have to be okay with having your name on their work.

You can find book ghostwriters online, but if you plan to hire one, be sure to ask for samples before you sign a contract. And never, ever pay for the book upfront. Instead, make an arrangement with the writer to pay them for each chapter as they produce it. That keeps them on schedule, and ensures that if they don't finish the project, you will at least have the work they did complete.

Learn to Write

Your other option is to learn to write. I'm convinced that anyone can learn to write if they practice. Take some local or online writing courses, or just sit down and start writing until you get better.

I wrote ten books before I published my first one.

Writing is a skill, and if you want to publish books, you will have to work to perfect it.

Decide on a Niche

Next, you need to decide whether you want to write non-fiction or fiction books — or both. It's possible to earn passive income streams from both types of books, and you should choose the one you will enjoy the most. That's because when you're racing against the clock to meet your deadline, you don't want it to feel as if you're pulling teeth.

To earn passive income from books, you will need to write a few books a year. The more books you have, the more your income will be. So, don't choose to write romance books just because you've heard that romance writers sell more books. They do. But if you don't enjoy what you're writing, readers aren't going to enjoy reading it.

So, decide on the types of books you want to write based on your interests and skill sets.

Sit Down and Write the Book

Your next step in the process is to outline the book[2]. For nonfiction and fiction alike, it makes it a lot easier if you prepare an outline before you start writing. When you're working from an outline, you won't waste time thinking about what you should write next, or searching the internet for your next point.

An outline is a guide that keeps you on track when writing a book and ensures that you hit all the major points.

Before you start writing, you should look at your outline and make sure you haven't left any questions unanswered. When someone buys your book, they do so because they believe it will answer their questions about a topic. And by outlining your book, you will ensure that it does.

---

2. https://www.rainmakerpress.com/my-musings/2018/7/25/how-to-outline-a-non-fiction-book

After you've outlined, it's time to start writing. And here's where a lot of people get hung up. I've heard from so many people that they haven't started their book because they don't have enough time that I wrote a book on the topic.

Trust me, if you really want to write a book, you will find the time. In fact, it's possible to write a book in a month only working on the weekend[3].

Here are some of my favorite methods to help you write faster:

- **Do time sprints.** This is my go-to whenever I'm working on a deadline and need to write fast. I find that if I set the timer for 30 minutes, and write as much as I can in that time frame, I can often write more than I can all day on other days. There's something about racing against the clock that gets the creative juices flowing.
- **Work in sections**. Another great way to trick your mind into writing faster is to work in sections. For example, you can tell yourself you will only write one scene or a chapter. When you do this, it not only focuses you on writing, but once you've come to the end of the scene or chapter, you will probably keep going.
- **Prelease the book.** A word of caution here: I use this method to ensure that I always have a book in progress, but unless you're a stickler for deadlines like I am, it could get you in trouble. Amazon and some of the other retailers allow authors to prerelease

---

3. https://goo.gl/FhHHOh

books about three months in advance. If you trust yourself enough to work quickly toward that deadline, it's a great way to ensure that you'll write. But the consequences for not meeting the deadline are severe, so only do this if you know 100 percent that you'll make the deadline.

Think of writing a book like this: most nonfiction books are only about ten chapters and 30,000 words. You should be able to easily write a chapter in a day or two. That means you can realistically write a book in month.

That's not so bad, is it?

Edit the Book

After you're satisfied with the book, you need to edit it. You can either edit the book yourself or hire a professional to do it for you. Most people recommend hiring a professional, but I am of a different mindset.

Most newbie writers don't have a huge budget to spend on their book, and I don't believe it's necessary to spend thousands of dollars to write a book. In fact, you can do it for under $100.

And one of the ways you can save is to edit the book yourself — or find a book editor who has rates you can afford.

If you choose to edit your book yourself, take the following steps:

- Print your book, and do a first edit on paper. Then make all the corrections in your computer document and print it again.

- Go over your book again and make any additional corrections that you see. Do this until you can read through the entire book without finding any errors.

- Use an online editing tool like Grammarly[4] to check for errors you may have missed. You can use the program for free is you only edit a portion of your book at a time. Make the suggestion corrections.

- Now print out your book again, but this time, read it out loud and make any corrections you find.

- Once you've made all the corrections, print out your book one more time and read it backwards. Start at the end and read it sentence-by-sentence. This will eliminate your brain's tendency to fill in words that you expect to be there — but really aren't.

If you don't want to edit the book yourself, you can always find an editor to do it for you who doesn't charge a lot of money. The best place to find these inexpensive editors is Kboards. They post their rates on the Writer's Café forum[5], and some will edit an entire book for $50 to $100. It's best to use one who has proven themselves with other writers on the forum.

Format the Book

After your book is written and edited, your next step is to format it in both an eBook and paperback version. Again, you have a couple of choices here.

- You can follow the somewhat confusing KDP guidelines[6] about formatting your eBook.
- You can download this free skeleton file[7] to create a beautiful books with very little effort. Just download it, and then insert your chapters into it one by one.
- Your next (and easiest) choice is to head over to fiverr[8] and look for a provider who formats eBooks and paperbacks. You'll pay about $5 for the service and have your book formatted in a day or so.
- Finally, you can upload a file to Draft to Digital[9] (D2D) and then download a variety of files, depending on where you plan to publish your book. For instance, to publish an eBook book on Amazon, you need a mobi file, and to publish it in paperback, you need a PDF file. You can download these and more from D2D.

Create a Book Cover

Next, you will need to create a book cover, but not just any book cover will do. I wish I could show you pictures of some horrible book covers on Amazon, but of course I can't do that.

But you know what I'm talking about.

---

6. https://kdp.amazon.com/en_US/help/topic/G200645680

7. https://www.dropbox.com/s/x3ztadnajckvpu7/
   Updated%20Skeleton%20File%20-%20NonFiction.docx?dl=0

8. https://www.fiverr.com/

9. https://www.draft2digital.com/

Book covers sell books, period. And in order to make a passive income stream from publishing books, you have to have good covers.

Here are your three choices when it comes to getting the perfect cover for your book.

- **Make it yourself for free.** I use canva.com to create some of my book covers. Just go to the site, create a free account, and use the book cover template to create yours. In fact, I created the covers on two of my best-selling books. But you have to have an eye for design in order to pull it off.
- **Buy a premade cover.** If you google premade covers, you will find a lot of sites that sell them. But one caveat: only buy one if you get exclusive rights to it. Otherwise, another author can use the same cover for their book.
- **Hire a cover designer.** Here's the truth, you don't have to pay a lot of money for a great book cover. I pay $30 for the covers I don't design myself. In fact, I'll give you my guy's info: Nathan Dasco — you can find him at nathanieldasco@gmail.com. You're welcome.

Upload the Book

Your next step in the process is to upload the book to the site you plan to sell from. For instance, if you're going to sell your book on Amazon (and you should), you will have to create a

KDP account, and upload the book according to their instructions.

Market the Book

Now that your book is for sale, it's time to tell the world about it. After all, you won't make passive income on it until people know it's there and begin to buy it.

And speaking of passive income, here's where it starts. So far, you've put some serious time into writing the book, formatting it, designing the cover, and uploading it.

But now that it's done, you will be able to sit back and begin collecting the royalties. So while you will have to do work in the beginning, the royalties you collect in the years to follow is passive.

Total Costs and Potential Earnings

I want to take a minute here to point some things out. Take a look at the following numbers and see for yourself why publishing books is a great way to earn passive income.

- Based on what I told you above, you can publish a book for under $100.
- The average indie author with one book sells 250 books. If you price your book at $2.99, that would net you about $2 a book after the site's commissions. That means your worst-case scenario is that you would make $500 profit. You typically start seeing better results after you publish your third book.

- But most indie's don't stop at one book. As you add to your catalog, your monthly income stream increases. In fact, authors who published 30 books or more often make at least $100,000 a year.

All of this possibility for less than $100 investment and some upfront work. Not bad, huh?

Chapter Nine: Become a Bank and Earn Passive Income

If you're looking for a way to earn a steady stream of passive income with almost no upfront work, you should know about peer-to-peer lending and crowdfunding.

We'll start with peer-to-peer lending.

How to Invest in Peer-in-Peer Lending

Here's how it works: When someone applies for a loan online at sites like Lending Club[1] or Prosper[2], their applications are examined just as they would be when applying for a bank loan. Their credit is checked, income tax returns are looked at to verify income, and they have to meet certain requirements to get a loan.

But instead of a bank giving them the money for their loan, investors do. In other words, if you decide to pursue this type of passive income stream, you will act as the lender. But you won't have to fund the entire loan to start investing.

You can invest as little as $25 per loan on both of these platforms, and then earn interest on them as a passive income stream.

---

1. https://www.lendingclub.com/

2. https://www.prosper.com/

Until recently, only accredited investors could earn passive income on peer-to-peer lending sites, but the law was changed in 2012, and now everyone can do it.

Here's what you need to do to invest in peer-to-peer lending.

Open an Account

Go to either Lending Club or Prosper and follow the instructions to set up an account. You must fund your Lending Club account with a minimum of $1,000 and your Prosper account with $25.

Not all states allow investors to use these platforms. The easiest way to find out if yours does is to try and set up an account with the site. It will ask for your zip code, and if your state isn't allowed, it won't let you go any further. (I'm not listing the states here because it constantly changes, and I don't want to give you bad information.)

Choose Your Loans

Next, you can choose the types of loans to fund. Each site categorizes the loans according to the borrower's credit history. They are scored from A to E, with an A rating being the highest credit score, and an E rating being a high-risk loan.

As the investor, it will be up to you to decide which types of borrowers you want to lend to.

The better the credit history, the less interest you will earn because you're not taking as big of a risk. Remember, the bigger risk you take, the more passive income you will earn. It's up to you to decide what kind of risk to take. At the time of this writing, the interest rates range from 5.99 percent to 36 percent. And the return on investment ranges from 5 to 8 percent.

You should know that not everyone repays their loans, and if you invest in one that isn't repaid, you will lose your investment.

To minimize your losses, invest small amounts in many different loans. For example, if you lose $25 on a class E loan, you could make up for with the four class A loans you invested in.

You can also allow the platform to choose your loans for you if you would rather not make the call yourself. This method is more passive because it doesn't require you to individually look at all of the loan applications to decide which one to invest in.

It all depends on your comfort level.

When you engage in automated investing, you will select your category: low, medium, and high-risk loans, and the platform will choose the loans for you.

Start Earning

Once you've invested, the platform will take about a 3 percent commission fee, leaving you with 97 percent of the interest earned on the loan. Obviously, the more money you invest in a platform, the more passive income you will earn.

Real Estate Crowdfunding

If you aren't ready to invest in a rental house, you can still earn a passive income stream from rentals by participating in real estate crowdfunding.

Over the years, crowdfunding has enabled many businesses to find the startup capital they needed, and borrowers to find loans when the banks wouldn't lend.

But real estate investing has been left behind. Unless you had some money socked away, you couldn't buy a rental house.

But now you have access to the real estate rental market for as little as $500. It's called real estate crowdfunding, and it's a game changer when it comes to earning passive income.

Here's how it works.

What is Real Estate Crowdfunding?

Real estate crowdfunding is a way for investors to invest in a portion of a commercial property. A commercial property is defined as a retail location, land, industrial, or a residential property such as multi-housing units.

Instead of going to the bank for a loan, the developer of the real estate property goes to a real estate crowdfunding platform and asks for the funding. Then the individuals who invest on the platform will decide whether they want to put their money toward that project.

Ultimately, the deal is funded with many small loans from investors, who then earn interest, as well as a percentage of their rental income (based on the amount invested), and if the property is sold, a percentage of the profit.

How to Invest in Real Estate Crowdfunding

Investing in real estate via a crowdfunding site is as easy as investing in peer-to-peer lending. You have several sites to choose from including PeerRealty.com and Fundrise. But they each have different minimums, and that makes a huge difference. For example, you will need $5,000 to start with PeerRealty[3], but only $500 to start investing with Fundrise[4].

Currently, all the talk is about Fundrise because of its easy-to-use platform and low entry investment amount.

To start with them, just go to the website and hit the sign up button. Instead of looking for individual properties to invest in, you will be asked to select a class of investments, and then the site will determine the best investments for you.

The site pays dividends quarterly. As of now, you can expect about a 10 percent return on investment, which beats most other investment vehicles. But keep in mind that even real estate investing can go bad and you can lose your money.

If you were looking for easy ways to earn passive income without a lot of upfront work, this chapter was probably ideal for you. Both peer-to-peer lending and real estate investing are excellent passive income streams, but they both require you to in-

---

3. https://peerrealty.com/

4. https://fundrise.com/

vest a good deal of money in order to earn a decent stream of income.

If you're looking for a passive income stream where you don't mind putting in a lot of work in the beginning for a potentially huge income stream that lasts for years, the next chapter might be of interest to you. In it, we'll talk about online courses, and how if you create the right one, you could easily earn enough passive income to quit the 9 to 5 for good.

Chapter Ten: The Set It and Forget It Passive Income Stream

By now, you've probably seen dozens of online courses. Heck, you may have even signed up for one. You can find online courses for just about anything you want, and people sign up for them like crazy.

But here's the thing about online courses: they take a lot of work to set up. But once you've done that, you can earn passive income from them for years. And I mean a lot of income.

A lot.

In fact, the online learning industry is expected to reach $240 billion by 2021. Do you want your piece of the pie? I know I do, which is why online courses will be my next passive income stream.

Do this one right, and you can earn a full-time income from it.

What are Online Courses?

While there are a lot of online courses online, not all of them are examples of what I'm talking about. Let me explain.

Many people read about how much money they can make with online courses, so they slap together a course in a day, and then upload it. They start dreaming of the day when they can fire their boss because they'll earn so much money from their e-course.

But that doesn't happen. Why?

Because people aren't dumb.

When someone creates a course only to make money and doesn't consider the people who will take the course, they are doomed from the start. With all the online courses out there, yours had better be good or else you will launch it to the sound of crickets.

I've watched over the years as people launch courses that don't contain much usable information and charge people thousands of dollars for them.

That's a shame, and it's not what I'm talking about here.

If you want to earn passive income from an online course, you will have to create a product that's so good it will continue selling long after it's published. Your students should get quality information that they can't find elsewhere in the format you present it in.

But it's going to take time. In fact, you should plan to spend about an hour for every finished five minutes of your course. Most people estimate that a successful course takes about 800 hours to complete.

But after that, you'll receive a passive income check for years, provided that you continue to update your course when needed and keep it in front of the public.

Before we talk about how to set up an online course and start making passive income, let's talk about the pros and cons of online courses.

The Pros of Online Courses

The pros definitely outweigh the cons in this one. Here are some of the benefits to creating an online course:

- Because of the e-course platforms I'll talk about below, setting up your course can be as simple as drop and drag.
- You can use online courses to expand an existing business. For example, if you blog, you can use them to offer readers more in-depth instruction.
- Once you create an online course, you can sell it over and over again. For years. And that's the very definition of passive income, isn't it?
- You can use an online course to funnel students into another product such as a more in-depth course or a pricy eBook you sell from your website.
- There are no time or geographical boundaries. Students can take your course at any hour and from anyplace in the world.

The Cons of Online Courses

There are some cons to online courses, but not nearly as many benefits.

- They take a lot of time to create.
- Because you will host your course on another

platform, you won't have control over some aspects of it.

- Your course must be something people want to learn or you won't earn any money from it.

How to Set Up an Online Course

Are you ready to put in some hard upfront work to secure your future with passive income? Here are the steps you will need to take to create and sell your online course.

Decide What You'll Teach

Your first step in creating an online course is to decide which topic you will teach. This might be easy for you if you specialize in an area and want to create the course around that. But you don't have to be an expert in anything to create an online course—you just have to be motivated, a great researcher, and willing to put in the work required to make it a quality course.

But you can choose from a niche that focuses narrowly, and one that is broader in scope.

- **Go the specialized route:** You can create a specialized course that won't appeal to as many people. These narrowly-focused courses are typically more expensive because the information can't be found just anywhere. Before you decide on this course, do some market research to determine if there are enough people interested in it.
- **Choose a more popular topic:** On the other hand, you can choose to create a course that many people

are interested in. Of course, if you go this route, you will have a lot of competition. But if you design a quality course and get it in front of the public, your chances of making a livable passive income are great.

Decide Where You Will Host Your Course

After you've decided what subject you want to teach, you need to look for a place to host your course. You have a lot of choices when it comes to hosting your online course, and I've listed the most popular platforms below. But don't stick to my list—feel free to research on your own in case I missed one that you prefer.

- Academy of Mine[1]: If a drop and drag platform is your goal, Academy of Mine may be the right one for you. It's easy to use comes with a lot of bells and whistles. Your price varies depending on how much you want to do yourself versus what you ask the site to do for you, but you should expect to pay $499 to $1,200 a month for this platform. You can sign up for a free 30-day trial.
- CourseCraft[2]: If you don't want a large monthly fee to cut into your passive income earnings, this platform might be better for you. You can start with a free membership plan that charges a 9 percent transaction fee instead of a monthly charge. You can use that for 100 students per month. And then once you start growing, you can upgrade to other plans

1. https://www.academyofmine.com/

2. https://coursecraft.net/

that range from $23 to $47 a month.

- LearnWorlds[3]: If you want to sell online courses from your own website, this platform allows you to do that. It provides you with everything you need, including payment gateways. You can expect to pay $24 to $249 per month, depending on which course package you buy.

- Ruzuku[4]: This platform has three different plans that allow you to choose from things like hosting the course on your own platform, zero transaction fees, and allowing students access to payment plans. You will pay $75 to $125 for this platform.

- Skillshare:[5] Even though this isn't a traditional online course platform, I'm including this in the list because it's another way to earn passive income by teaching. With this platform, you create a 30 to 40 minute course, upload it, and then are paid every time someone watches it. The site claims that some of its teachers earn as much as $100,000 from their courses. It's definitely worth checking out.

- Teachable[6]: This is one of the most popular online course platforms, and one you should definitely consider. You will pay $29 to $399, depending on which plan you choose. All plans offer unlimited students.

- Thinkific[7]: You can create your online course under

3. https://www.learnworlds.com/

4. https://www.ruzuku.com/

5. https://www.skillshare.com/

6. https://teachable.com/

your own brand with platform. Monthly plans range from $49 to $499, and all include unlimited students.

- Udemy:[8] This is probably one of the most well-known online course platforms, and it's where you will find the most students. You won't pay a monthly fee, but to host your course here, you will pay a hefty 50 percent commission fee if the student finds you on their platform, and a lower commission that's based on a sliding scale if you bring them.

After you've chosen which site you will host your online course on, it's time to begin designing it. This is where the real work begins.

But each platform listed above not only has different requirements, but allow you to do different things to make your course unique. For instance, some allow you to upload PDFs to provide to your students, while others let you create slide shares or fillable workbooks.

That means I can't give you a play-by-play instruction guide to creating your online course. So, I've listed a general overview below that contains enough information to get you started. Then you can alter your course depending on the platform's requirements.

Here are the steps you will need to take:

Outline Your Course

7. https://www.thinkific.com/

8. https://www.udemy.com/

Your first step in preparing your course is to outline it. Much like you do a book, you need to have a detailed outline that guides the course. And if you already have a book, the process will be easier because you have an outline of sorts.

For this process, you should step into the shoes of your student. Think of your outline as guiding them through the information you are going to teach them in a chronological order.

Here are the steps you should take to create a good course outline:

- **Brainstorm your course:** Start by making a list of everything you plan to include in your course. Don't worry about keeping order at this point—just jot down everything that comes to your mind.
- **Now put it on order:** adjust your list so that it's in the order the student needs to learn it. Make sure that for every new topic you introduce, the student has learned the knowledge they need to understand it in a previous lesson.
- **Arrange it:** Now it's time to arrange the content into chapters and subsections. Create main chapters, and then include each subject under it that goes with that topic. For example, if you are creating a course on vegan eating, one of your chapters may be about what to avoid. The subsections under that chapter could be foods, clothing, condiments, ingredients, and so on.
- **Organize it:** Finally, go section by section and determine how you will relate the information to your students. You should use videos on some

sections, PDF's on others, slide shows on some, quizzes, and screen recordings on others. Keep it interesting to keep your student's attention.

Write the Course

Now that you have a clear picture of where you want to take your course, it's time to write it. This is the most labor intensive part of the process, and you should plan on spending some serious time with it. But as you're pouring yourself into it, keep reminding yourself of the years of passive income you will earn as a result of these upfront efforts.

Upload Your Course

When you've created the best course you can, it's time to upload it to your platform. The hard work is over, and if you've chosen the right course, uploading it should be a breeze.

But if you can't quite figure out how to do it, be sure to check out Fiverr and look for someone who has experience in that platform.

And keep in mind that you own the rights to your course, so you can upload it to as many platforms as you want. For example, you can host it on your own website for the people on your email list, and upload it to Udemy to take advantage of the huge amount of students who visit the site every day.

Market Your Course

Now it's time to get the word out about your online course. This step is important because if people don't know your course exists, you will never create a source of passive income from it.

Get Some Reviews

E-courses are just like eBooks—students won't look at them unless they have a few reviews. So, you need to give away your course to at least ten people in exchange for a review. Social proof is an important part of getting people to take a chance on your course.

Listen to the Feedback

After the test students take your course, ask them for feedback. Ask if they wish you had included anything that didn't, or if there is anything else they would change about the course. Listen carefully to the feedback, and make changes to the course if you hear the same feedback more than once—or if you believe it will make your course better.

Send an email

If you have an email list, now is the time to tell them about your course. It's as good as it's going to be, and you can confidently offer the course to your fan base.

Use Social Media

Send an announcement out over social about your e-course, and ask your friends and family to do the same. You can also use Facebook ads to get your course in front of the people who are most likely to buy it. The more people who see, the more students you'll gain.

Useful Tools

Finally, I want to leave you with a few tools that you will help you complete your course.

- OBS Studio[9]: If you want to record video for your course using freeware, this is a great choice because it don't put a watermark on your video.
- Camtasia[10] or ScreenFlow[11]: These software programs allow you to make screenshots for both Windows and Mac.
- LCDS[12] and Courselab[13]: both of these software programs help you create your course and then integrate it.

That's a lot of work isn't it? But my guess is that if you put in the upfront work, you won't even remember it as you're earning enough passive income a couple years from now to quit your job.

---

9. https://obsproject.com/

10. https://www.techsmith.com/video-editor.html

11. https://screenflow.en.softonic.com/mac

12. https://www.microsoft.com/en-us/learning/lcds-tool.aspx?utm_campaign=elearningindustry.com&utm_source=%2Ffree-authoring-tools-for-elearning&utm_medium=link#tab1

13. http://www.courselab.com/view_doc.html?mode=home

But if you don't want to put in as much upfront work, let's talk about something in the next chapter that takes little to no up-front work, but can still produce an enormous amount of passive income.

Chapter Eleven: Earn Passive Income for the Future

In this chapter, we're going to talk about how to earn passive income, month after month, without doing a thing.

I'm talking about investing in the stock market with an aim for long-term growth. Think compound interest.

Investing in dividends and retirement accounts is a great way to earn passive income, but only if you approach it in a methodical way that plans for the long term.

And don't worry if you don't have a lot of money to invest. What I'm talking about in this chapter is investing a small amount into dividends or (preferably and) a Roth 401K and then sitting back and watching your money double, triple, quadruple in value.

And it's all because of the magic of compound interest. I defined the term earlier in this book, but now I'd like to spend a little more time on it. Trust me, when it really sinks in, it will change the way you think about money.

What is Compound Interest?

Did you know that Albert Einstein called compound interest the eighth wonder of the world? That's not surprising when you learn how it can not only provide you with passive income, but set you up to retire early or live like a king or queen when you do retire.

Here's how it works: when you take out a loan for a house or a car, you are borrowing someone else's money. And because you have use of it instead of them, they charge you interest for it. We all understand that that's the cost of borrowing money.

But when you invest in stocks or dividends, you are loaning someone else your money. You are buying an interest in the stock or dividend, and so *you* are paid interest.

And if you're smart, you will set up your investments so that you're not only paid interest on the principle, but on the accumulating interest and dividends as well.

For example, if you invest $100 in dividends and receive $10 in dividends the next quarter, you can do one of the two things: you can reinvest the $10 and the next quarter be paid interest on $110, or you can take out the $10 every quarter and continue to only earn interest on the $100.

That may not seem like a big deal now, but compound interest accumulates quickly and if you reinvest it, your $100 will turn into hundreds of thousands of dollars over the years.

Here's a graph to illustrate the magic of compound interest:

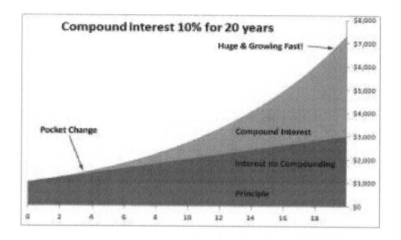

Do you see how compound interest can make your investments grow substantially more than simple interest?

Here's a real life example: imagine that you invest $10,000 in a stock and it pays out 7 percent interest a year. If you leave it in untouched for 30 years, compound interest would magically convert that $10,000 into just over $80,000.

And if you left it in for another 10 years — 40 in total — you would have about $160,000 in the account.

Talk about the perfect passive income setup.

While it's true that you couldn't touch the money for some years, that doesn't take away from the fact that as you go about your life, compound interest is doing the work for you and building a hefty nest egg.

There are two methods of using the stock market to earn passive income that I'll cover in this chapter: dividends and IRAs.

How to Earn Passive Income with Dividends

Did you know that some stocks pay dividends when you buy them? It's true, many of the S&P 500 stocks send out quarterly checks to the people who own their stocks. If that's not passive income, I don't know what is.

But if you truly want to make passive income from dividends, you won't cash those checks. Let's talk about how to best use dividends to earn passive income.

What are Dividends?

Companies pay dividends for three reasons.

- It makes so much money that it can't reinvest all of it back into the company, so it sends dividend checks to the people who own its stocks. This is called a residual dividend policy.
- To make their stock more appealing to investors, some companies pay a percentage of their quarterly or annual earnings to investors via dividends routinely. This is called a stable dividend.
- Some companies do both — they pay a stable dividend and also pay special dividends when it experiences positive growth.

Where Do I Find Stocks That Pay Dividends?

The Investor Junkie does a great job of updating their list[14] year-ly with all the S&P 500 stocks that have paid dividends regu-larly for the past 25 years.

Bu I am not a stock expert, so please don't take my advice when it comes to choosing your stocks. Your best bet is to talk to a professional and let them guide your choices.

Why Dividends Make Great Passive Income Investments

The secret lies in the compound interest. You see, when you reinvest the dividends that these stocks pay you, you will in-crease the magic of compound interest. Because you will not only earn compound interest on the principle balance and in-terest that you've earned so far, but you will also earn it on the dividends.

It's a win-win, and if you want passive income that requires no work but yields a significant amount of money, you should def-initely look into dividends.

But there is another way to use the stock market to earn passive income.

Roth IRAs

I can't talk about passive income and not mention Roth IRAs. If you start young enough, you can invest as little as $100 a month, and retire a millionaire. All for doing nothing more than writing a check or hitting "send" once a month to transfer money into your Roth IRA account.

Here's how it works.

You can contribute $6,000 to a Roth IRA per year if you're under 55. And because of compound interest, that money will grow in the same way a dividend will. For example, if you invested the maximum of $6,000 a year for 25 years and gained an average 8 percent return, you would have $475,000. (But you would have only put in $150,000) That's a $375,000 profit for doing absolutely nothing.

And because a Roth IRA is considered a post-tax investment, you would not pay any taxes on it when you withdrew your money — you've already paid them.

This makes a Roth IRA a great way to save passive income — or invest it. Let me explain.

Multiply Your Other Passive Income Streams with a Roth IRA

If you earn passive income from another stream — say rental houses — you can invest that passive money into your Roth IRA and let it grow — by earning tax-free compound interest.

It's a way to multiply your passive income streams exponentially.

How to Set Up a Roth IRA

You have a few choices when it comes to setting up an IRA. You can consult with a traditional financial planner and they can go over your options. They know the rules for every IRA, and can guide you to the right one.

Or, you could use a robo-investor. These robo-investors are gaining popularity. Sites like Betterment[15] and SoFi[16] offer investment advice based on computer algorithms. They will help you choose your risk factor and some will even automatically adjust it as you age.

It just doesn't get any simpler than that.

Are you ready to dive deep into our last passive income stream? We're going to talk about an aspect of blogging that can bring in a sizable income stream *if* you put in the upfront work.

---

15. https://www.betterment.com/

16. https://www.sofi.com/

Chapter Twelve: Blog Your Way to Passive Income

Surely, you've heard by now that it's possible to start a blog and earn a lot of money from it. But blogging isn't passive. Trust me, I started my blog[1] a year ago, and can barely keep up with it.

But certain aspects of your blog are passive, and that's what I want to talk to you about today. But first, let's talk about some assumptions. In other words, certain things need to be true before you can begin earning significant passive income on your blog.

- You should have about 100,000 visitors to your blog every day. That's a lot of visitors, and most experts believe that it takes about two years of posting excellent articles consistently to get that many people to your site every day.
- You should have a large list of email subscribers who read and engage with your emails. Under 5 percent of your email list will open the messages you send, so you need a large list.
- You need to build a relationship with your followers. Answer their emails, interact with them in the comments, and talk to them like real people in your blog posts.

---

1. https://www.rainmakerpress.com/

Once you have established the above requirements, you're ready to earn some passive income from your blog. But keep in mind that this is an upfront type of passive income. You may have to work two years in order to get your blog to the place where you can start earning passive income streams from it.

That's exactly what I'm doing with mine. And I have about a year-and-a-half to go!

Here are some real passive income streams you can earn once your blog is established:

You Can Sell Digital Products

Most bloggers sell at least one product on their blog. You can sell something you created like an app, an eBook, or a proprietary system.

If you decide to sell digital products, you will need to have a delivery system plus a shopping cart system installed on your blog so you can take payments. You can market the products to your email list, with Facebook ads, or if you have a good number of people visiting your blog, make sure the products tab is clearly defined on your site so they will find it.

And you don't have to wait until you hit 100,000 visitors to begin this blog passive income stream. My blog isn't nearly that popular, but I offer some products for writers and entrepreneurs that do okay. And as it becomes visited more frequently, the sales will increase.

You Can Use Drop Shippers

If you want to sell physical products, but you don't want the hassle of storing them and shipping them out yourself, use drop shippers. These third-party vendors store the products for you, and then when someone orders from your site, they ship the product out. And the sites connect to your website so they are notified the moment a customer places an order.

You can use vendors like Teespring[2] or Printful[3] to create custom print-on-demand tee-shirts, mugs, towels, backpacks, hoodies, phone covers, and more. You come up with the design, and they will print it and ship it to the customer when it's ordered.

Add Affiliate Links to Your Website

You know how when you're reading a blog, and the blogger suddenly starts talking about a product and gives you a link to it? Most likely, they are referring you to a product that, if you buy it, they will earn a commission from.

Many bloggers earn a lot of money from affiliate links. But you can't just use your blog to promote anything. Only offer the products and services that you know and trust, and your readers will thank you for it. Affiliate income is a great way to earn passive income, but it must be done honestly and carefully.

You can sign up for affiliates one of two ways: approach the company directly or go through an affiliate aggregator.

How to Sign Up for Affiliates Directly

2. https://community.teespring.com/

3. https://www.printful.com/

Not every product offers a direct affiliate program, and the best way to find out if the product of your choice does is to visit their website. Scroll down to the bottom of the site and look for an affiliate link. If you find a link, click on it and follow the instructions from the site about how to apply to be an affiliate.

If you don't see one, try looking for it at one of the sites I talk about below.

How to Find Affiliates Using an Aggregator

You can find thousands of affiliate opportunities on aggregators. These sites list a lot of different affiliate programs that you can apply for from one place.

Here are a list of the most popular ones:

- ShareASale[4]
- CJ Affiliate[5]
- FlexOffers[6]
- JVZoo[7]
- ClickBank[8]

Keep in mind that you won't automatically be accepted for every affiliate that you try to sign up for. Many affiliates only want to work with bloggers who have enough traffic to their site to justify the arrangement. But it is possible to get some af-

4. https://www.shareasale.com/

5. https://www.cj.com/

6. https://www.flexoffers.com/

7. https://www.jvzoo.com/

8. https://www.clickbank.com/

filiate approvals when just starting out, and then get approved for the bigger ones once you build traffic.

Start an Email Course or Challenge

Finally, you can create passive income by starting an email course or other daily challenge or series. An email course is different than the type of online course we spoke about in an earlier chapter. That kind of course is hosted on a website. But an email course is sent out via email. It's completely passive after you spend the upfront time to create it.

And you can send your visitors things other than courses. You can do a 30-day challenge, 30-days of inspirational writings, or anything else you can think of.

Is a Blog Right for You?

Blogging is definitely not passive income, but it is possible to create passive income streams that stem from the efforts you put into your blog.

Now It's Time to Make a Plan

I've given you a lot to think about, haven't I? I've told you about purely passive income streams, passive income streams that require a little upfront work, and those that require a lot. But each of the streams I've talked about in this book have the potential to bring you good enough income streams to replace your 9 to 5 if that's your goal.

The next steps are up to you. Will you take the information and use it to create a new life, or will you set this book aside and forget about it in a day or two?

You are the only one who can create passive income and change your life. I promise you, taking the necessary steps now will pay off big in the years to come.

Don't live with regrets. Instead, make the commitment to take the first step toward a better life today.

The Work from Home Series

How to Work From Home and Make Money: 10 Proven Home-Based Businesses You Can Start Today (Work from Home Series: Book 1)

Life is Too Short to Work for Someone Else!

Are you tired of struggling just to get by with a paycheck that doesn't quite stretch far enough? Or are you one of the millions of people who are out of work in an economy gone bad? Maybe you long to be your own boss so you can set your own schedule and choose the path your life will take.

---

1. https://www.amazon.com/gp/product/B01CTMI7R4/ref=series_rw_dp_sw

Whatever it is that brought you to this page, you're obviously looking for answers. **The good news is you've come to the right place.**

I've spent the past 20 years working for myself, and I would never dream of punching another clock or trudging to someone else's office every day to collect a meager paycheck. That's because I've discovered the secret: when you work for yourself, you're happier, more productive, and you have unlimited earning potential.

After all, **why would you want to work so hard to fund someone else's dreams?**

Working for myself has allowed me to live a lifestyle that many people can only dream about. I have the flexibility to create the life I want, take days off when I need to, and I decide how much money I make by choosing the hours I work.

But don't be fooled. Working from home at a home-based business isn't easy. It takes hard work and dedication to build a successful business that will make money.

In my book, I'm pleased to offer you **10 proven, realistic ways to work from home and earn a great income.** And I won't just offer you a brief explanation of each method like some other books do.

In each chapter, I provide you with the information and facts you need to determine if that business is right for you. But I don't stop there. I'll also give you important links and resources, so if you decide you want to pursue one of the home-based business ideas listed in this book, **you'll have everything you need to begin.**

So, the choice is yours. Will you wake up tomorrow morning and spend your day funding someone else's dream, or will you finally take the steps needed to claim your own success?

Why not start right now by buying How to Work From Home and Make Money? It's one of the most important things you'll do to begin the process of achieving your own dreams.

Click here to go to Amazon and buy the book![2]

How to Build a Writing Empire in 30 Days or Less (Work from Home Series: Book 2)

Do You Want to Make a Real Living as a Writer? You'll Have to Throw Out Everything You Know

Let me guess—you're a talented writer who is willing to do whatever it takes to make a full-time living by writing. You've read countless articles and books on the subject, followed the suggestions in them, but you just can't seem to make the income leap.

Or you may be a new writer who is convinced that you're missing something because your own experience isn't matching up to what you've read is possible.

Or perhaps you've been moonlighting as a freelance writer for years, and you're convinced that it's simply not possible to quit your "real" job and do what you love full time.

Let me tell you a secret. You've been lied to. Yes, you heard me correctly. **Lied. To.**

The truth is, only about 10 percent of writers earn enough working full time to support themselves. *Ten percent.* That's not something all those other how-to writing books spend a lot of time on, is it?

Luckily, there's a real solution.

I know this because I've been doing it myself for years. But in order to be successful in this business, you'll have to turn the current freelance writing working model on its head. In fact, you pretty much **have to throw everything you thought you knew out the window.**

What I'm talking about is a new system. One that doesn't limit a freelance writer's ability to make a great income because of time constraints. I'm talking about earning a living anyone would be proud of.

In this book, I'll show you how to create your own Writing Empire in 30 days or less. You'll learn:

- Why most freelancers can't make a decent living—and what to do about it
- How to structure your writing business in a way that works best for your lifestyle

- How to brand your business to attract the type of clients you want
- Where to find clients and how to land the jobs
- How to structure your time in order to earn the highest possible income in the shortest amount of time
- How to hire a team of qualified, motivated writers who will help you build your Empire

And that's not all. I'll give you a **step-by-step plan** that will lead you to success. This plan looks **in detail** at your first:

- Day
- Week
- Month
- And beyond

Like I said, I structured my own business this way, so let my experience help you achieve your dreams.

Are you ready to get serious about your writing career and make some serious money? Start right now by downloading the book and learn how to make a real living with writing!

Click here to buy the book on Amazon![3]

---

3. https://goo.gl/C5Eiq7

How to Publish a Book on Amazon: Real Advice from Someone Who's Doing It Well (Work from Home Series: Book 5)

Are you tired of "how to publish books" that are full of fluff and no real information? So was I.

Before I began my publishing career with Kindle books, I read just about everything out there, looking for real answers to questions I had about the industry. But much to my disappointment, most of the books were filled with fluff or stories of people who "hit it big" without really telling me how or why.

I determined to jump in and learn for myself—and that's exactly what I did. I started with my first book, How to Work from Home and Make Money, and then quickly published three more. I was looking for the topic of my fifth book when it hit me—**why not share what I've learned with the people who still haven't made the leap and published their own book?**

It all began when I received an email from a book promotion site. One of the features was a how to book about publishing Kindle books, so out of curiosity, I followed the link and read the reviews. And sure enough, the page was full of people complaining that the book didn't contain any valuable information.

So here's what I decided to do. Write a book that answers all of the real questions without painting an unrealistic view of the possibilities. I answer things like:

- How to pick book topics that will sell. (Why it's important, and what I've done right—and wrong.)
- How to write a book in 30 days or less. (And take weekends off)
- How to conduct research for your book.
- How to make your own covers for free.
- The pros and cons of pre-releasing your book.
- When you should enroll your book in Kindle Unlimited (And when you shouldn't.)
- How to format your book yourself. (Including the clickable table of contents) And how to get it done for cheap if you don't want to.
- Why you need a paperback version. (And how to create one)
- Why you may need an audio book (And how to get one for free)
- How to get your book translated into other

languages for free (And why you should)

- Why ranking matters (And what to do if your book isn't ranking well.)
- How to market your book. (Including links and contact information for the people I use)
- What to do after you publish your first book.
- How much you can REALLY expect to make with Kindle publishing

I talk about the mistakes I've made so you don't make them, too. And I provide you with **step-by-step instructions and relevant links for all of the above areas**—and more. In other words, this book is the ONLY book you'll need to start a career publishing Kindle books.

If you've been dreaming of publishing a book, but don't know where to start—or if you've already published but can't find success—this may be the book you've been waiting for.

Why not take the first step toward your publishing career and download it right now? I promise you won't find any fluff or useless information in it. Just an actionable guide that answers the questions no one else will.

Click here to buy the book from Amazon![1]

How to Start a Home-Based Food Business: Turn Your Foodie Love into Serious Cash with a Food Business Startup (Work from Home Series Book 3)

1

Finally, a Comprehensive Guide to Starting a Food Business!

Do your insides jump for joy when you see a perfectly frosted cupcake or cookie? Or do you love the look of violet lavender syrup or a mouthwatering strawberry and lime jam? Or are you more of a savory person and melt when you see a jar of homemade salsa or seasoned nuts with just the right amount of spices?

If food excites you as much as it does me, you just might be a foodie. And in today's food-centered world, there is serious money to be made with your passion.

Food consumption has really changed in the past decade, and now more than ever, people want to know what's in their food, where it came from and who made it. That's bad news for businesses that mass produce food, but great news for those in the cottage food industry.

You see, in the past individuals who wanted to sell food were required to involve the state health inspectors and lease commercial kitchens in order to sell to the public. Obviously, that prevented a lot of people from pursuing their food dreams. But now many states have passed **cottage food laws** that are designed to give home chefs and bakers the right to produce products from their homes and sell them to the public.

If you've read my other books, you know I'm a serial entrepreneur. I've opened and closed many businesses in my lifetime, and there's nothing I love more than taking an idea and turning it into a smoothly run, profitable business. And this book was born of that desire.

Let me explain.

I bake. There—it's out in the open. I'm a guy and I bake. Can we please move on?

Specifically, I bake specialty brownies that are so good I've had local stores approach me and ask me to sell them wholesale, and I get phone calls from friends begging me to bake a batch. Yeah, my brownies are that good.

So when I heard about the changes in the law allowing people to start home-based food businesses, my entrepreneurial mind starting spinning. I have a great product, so in my mind, there was no reason why I couldn't create a profitable business. I should just open one, right?

Fortunately, that's not the way I roll. I have never simply opened a business and learned as I go—instead I conduct so much research that I know absolutely everything there is to know before I begin. In other words, I leave no room for error. I want the information up front so I can make the best decisions and build a successful business.

Otherwise, what's the point?

So, when the idea of opening a cottage food business occurred to me, I began researching and I didn't stop for months. That's where this book comes in. There is a lot to know about this type of business, and one thing I learned is that there is simply nowhere that you can get all of the information in one place.

Until this book.

Don't believe me? Take a look at all the other books on the subject and just see if the author provides a state-by-state index of all the cottage food laws. Let me save you some time. They don't.

And recipes that fit into the guidelines of the laws? Nope, you won't find them in other books. How about serious insight into how to best brand, package and market your home-based food business? You'll only find that in this book.

So, let my obsessive research into business ideas, along with my entrepreneurial skills, help you in your own business. I've done the hard work for you, so **all you have do is follow the plan I've outlined in this book and you'll be on your way to building your very own food business**. And all the newbie questions you have but are too embarrassed to ask? I had them, too and I've included the answers to them in this book.

If you're ready to pursue your foodie dreams, download the book and learn everything you need to know!

<u>Click here to buy the book on Amazon!</u>[2]

---

2. https://www.amazon.com/gp/product/B01HX058Y2/
   ref=series_rw_dp_sw

How to Brand Your Home-Based Business: Why Business Branding is Crucial for Even the Smallest Startups (Work from Home Series Book 4)

How to

Your Home-Based Business

Sam Kerns

What's the Difference Between a Successful Home-Based Business and One that Fails? Branding.

Home-based business startups are exploding all across the world as more and more people realize that the best way to take control of your life—and your finances—is to work for yourself. But what many people forget to do is brand their small business.

That's a mistake. You see, business branding isn't only for the big guys. Home-based business owners also need to focus on creating a brand that will speak to their customers and forge that ever-important bond between the business and the public.

But home-based business owners shouldn't play by the same rules when it comes to branding their business. For starters, most solopreneurs don't have the finances to pay big shot logo designers, graphic artists and copywriters, not to mention the cash to invest in top-notch packaging and marketing efforts.

And why would you want to?

Building a brand doesn't have to be expensive or complicated, but it does require a plan and the knowledge about how to best create the right brand and then use it to build your business.

If you own a home-based business and can't figure out why you're not meeting your goals, could it be that you haven't take the time to properly brand it? And if you're just starting out, you shouldn't even think about opening your doors until you've branded your business for success.

In this book, I'll show you:

- What branding is and why your business can't truly succeed without it
- The biggest benefits you'll reap from a business brand

- The 7 mistakes most people make when building a brand—and how to avoid them
- How to build a brand in today's high-tech world
- A step-by-step guide to brand building that will work for any type of business (along with links and resources)

Don't let your hard work go to waste. Increase your market share (and profits) in your current home-based business, or start your new business on the right foot by reading this important book.

Click Here to Buy The Book from Amazon![1]

---

1. https://goo.gl/6flLFo

The Writer's Toolkit Boxed Set (Work from Home: Books 2 and 5)

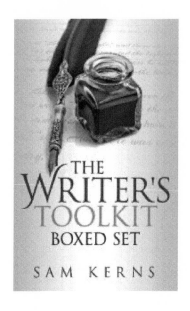

Two bestselling books in one boxed set!

Click here to buy the boxed set from Amazon![1]

---

1. https://goo.gl/hKKhsG

The Weekend Writer: How to Write a Non-Fiction Book in Two Months even if You Have a Full-Time Job (Work from Home Series: Book 6)

Do you fear you'll never publish a book because you don't have time to write?

Let me guess—you're a writer, but so far, the book you *know* will be a big hit is stuck inside your head because you simply don't have the time to sit down and write it. You've probably been told that you need to block out mass chunks of time to write a book, but I'm here to tell you that's just not true.

It's possible to write a quality book in two months—writing only on the weekends—using my step-by-step plan.

I'm not talking about putting out some of the junk that passes for books these days. I'm talking about writing a full-length book you'll be proud to put your name on, and readers will be thrilled they bought.

Here's what you'll find in this revolutionary book:

- How to get in the right mindset to write on a limited schedule
- How to choose your book topic so it sells
- How to outline your book in a way that makes writing it easier
- How to set up a no-fail writing schedule so you can meet your deadline
- How to use productivity hacks that will help you stay on track and accomplish your goal
- How to edit as you go
- A weekend-by-weekend guide that shows you the exact steps you need to take to have a finished book in just two months—only writing on the weekends.

Click here to buy the book from Amazon![1]

---

1. https://goo.gl/FhHHOh

How to Relaunch Your Book: Use this 7-Step Proven Program to Bring Your Book Back to Life (Book 7)

Do You Have a Book That Isn't Selling? Don't Leave Money on the Table!

There's nothing more exciting than writing and publishing a book, but if you're like most authors, your book sells for the first couple of months and then quietly and alarmingly sinks to the bottom of Amazon's rankings. Or maybe your book never saw success. There are thousands of book authors who thought their book would achieve success only to watch it sink to the bottom of the rankings. Sadly most book authors simply accept that it's just the way things are.

But it doesn't have to be.

The truth is, **it is possible to relaunch your book months—or even years—after its initial release and see success.** To prove this, I'll use the first book in my Work from Home series, and relaunch it as an example of the process I outline in this book. I purposefully allowed the book to slip in the rankings so I could use it as a case study for this book. But keep in mind that I'm certain the program works because I've used it many times.

A successful book relaunch is more complicated than simply marketing your book again. In fact, to do it successfully, you'll need to follow the 7-step program I outline in this book. Some of the things we'll cover are how to:

- Analyze your book's position
- Create an improvement roadmap
- Test the existing cover to determine whether or not to design a new one
- Rearrange your book categories using my Lift Off strategy
- Ensure your internal marketing techniques are in place to increase sales of other books in the series
- Use the relaunch to increase the size of your mailing list
- Organize the relaunch so that you don't experience another quick drop off in sales.

This book not only provides you with a 7-step process, but I'll also give you an "over the shoulder" look at how I successfully follow the program myself.

If you have books on Amazon that aren't selling, you're leaving money on the table. Why should your only option be continuously writing new books to make money on Amazon? The secret is that you can—and should—revive your old books. Won't you follow along as I show you how to bring your backlist to life and reignite those book sales?

Buy the Book on Amazon Now![1]

---

1. https://goo.gl/QvWWvr

The 30 Day Small Business Startup Plan: Do You Have What it Takes to Be Your Own Boss? (The Work from Home Series: Book 8)

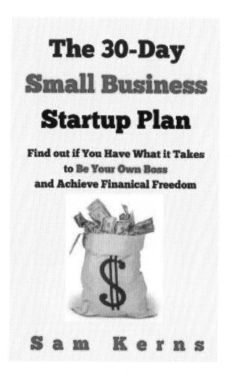

In this myth-busting book, bestselling author Sam Kerns, strips away the falsehoods surrounding entrepreneurship and challenges you to do a bare, in-your-face analysis of whether starting a business is the right move for you.

The truth is, not everyone is cut out to be their own boss. Entrepreneurship is hard, and unless you approach your new business with a solid understanding of how you will react to the stresses and challenges, you can't really know how you'll do. In addition, there are some basic skills you must have to run a successful business, and without them, you don't have a chance.

Does that sound harsh? Here's the reality:

- One out of every two business fail within the first year according to the Small Business Association.
- That same report shows that one-third of those new businesses fail in the first two years.
- The US Bureau of Labor and Statistics says that only half of new businesses that make it to the five year mark survive.

But what if I told you there is a way to determine whether or not you are cut out to be your own boss—and **increase your odds of becoming a success?** What if you could know if quitting your job and starting your own business is the right move for you—*before* you took the leap?

And if you find out that you don't have what it takes? I'll teach you how to get past your limitations and increase your odds of success.

You see, I talk to way too many people who left their jobs to venture out on their own before they were ready. And if you ask them, they'll all tell you the same thing: They wish they'd been better prepared so their great business idea didn't result in a missed opportunity.

In other words, if they had the information outlined in this book *before* they started their own business, they might have succeeded.

If you like the idea of starting your own business and want the best chance for success, you'll love the hard-hitting and practical advice found in *The Work from Home 30 Day Challenge*.

Don't take the most important step of your life without first evaluating your position. Buy The 30 Day Work from Home Challenge now to give yourself a better chance for success!

<u>Buy the Book on Amazon!</u>[1]